ANTONIO COLLAZO

A TRUE APOSTLE

ANTONIO COLLAZO
A TRUE APOSTLE

Wilfredo Estrada Adorno

Prologue by
Esdras Betancourt

ediciones
GUARDARRAYA

Orlando, FL

2017

ANTONIO COLLAZO
A TRUE APOSTLE

All rights reserved © 2017 Wilfredo Estrada Adorno
ISBN: 978-1986539432
Library of Congress Number: 2017960484

First Edition

Printed in the United States

Translated by Benjamin Pérez
Editor: Wilfredo Estrada Adorno
Art design: Jonathan Miranda

This volume is dedicated with sincere appreciation

To

Pérsida Lugo Collazo

(Sister Persis)

Faithful and loyal companion of Reverend Antonio
Collazo

for fifty-two years of marriage and fruitful ministry

Table of Contents

Acknowledgements

I must begin by expressing my sincere appreciation to the Collazo-Lugo family for their support and collaboration in making this work possible. Writing a biography of a true giant of the faith, as was Reverend Antonio Collazo, requires much collaboration. My special thanks to Pérsida Lugo Collazo and the Collazo children, Ligia, Juan Antonio (Totoño), Pérsida (Tita), Raquel, and Rebecca (Tata) for the enthusiastic support they gave to this project.

Special thanks to Reinaldo Burgos and Noemí González for taking time to review the first draft. To José Raúl Febus invaluable help in reviewing the final draft and editing the footnotes. However, any grammatical or typographical error in the book is my sole responsibility. I offer my thanks also to Jonathan Miranda for his cover art and for preparing the work for publication.

Special appreciation also goes to Yamitza López, my administrative assistant for the last year and a half, for transcribing many interviews and articles.

I owe a special debt of gratitude to the many persons close to Reverend Collazo who graciously afforded me the opportunity for interviews. Their reflections on the impact Brother Tony had on their lives and ministry is at the heart of this book.

My deepest gratitude goes to my wife Carmen who walked with me throughout the research for this project, and for giving of her time so that I could dedicate myself to its writing and editing. As always, I am grateful to my three sons and daughter and their families for joining me on this journey that is so important to all of us.

Finally, to those I cannot name who were part of this pilgrimage, my sincerest thanks for your encouragement along this interesting journey of hope. To all of you, a thousand thanks!

Wilfredo Estrada Adorno
September 10, 2017
The date that Hurricane Irma struck
the state of Florida

Prologue

Upon reading Dr. Wilfredo Estrada Adorno's detailed biography of a true Apostle, as is the case with Reverend Antonio Collazo, a veritable photo album of memories going back to my childhood flashed through my mind. The first picture is from the Dominican Republic where the Apostle of Pentecost Juan L. Lugo and Bible teacher Johnny Pérez visited my house. My father, Ángel Betancourt, was the missionary of the Pentecostal Church of God in that country and Lugo served as Superintendent of the work in Puerto Rico. Later, as indicated in this biography, Tony Collazo (the name by which many of us identified him) married Pérsida Lugo Ortiz thus becoming Reverend Lugo's son-in-law. It was clearly God's plan to bring these two men together in much the same way as He did with Paul and Barnabas.

The second picture is from Puerto Rico. There I saw Antonio Collazo as a pastor and National Superintendent. His manner, both as a Christian and servant-leader, were examples that later influenced my own ministry. Many of my mental pictures of Brother Tony revolve around his ministry as Pastor of the Church at the Parada 22 in Santurce, Puerto Rico. many events of the Church of God *Mission Board* were held there. However, the picture that left the greatest impression on me was his work as Overseer. He led the pastor's conferences and conventions with the wisdom of Solomon, with gentleness, and with firmness.

Opening the picture album once again, I see the Hispanic neighborhood in New York City. Here we see how God is preparing the ministry trajectory of this young man who had been called to serve in His vineyard. Brother Tony accepted the Lord as Savior at age eight in Puerto Rico. In 1928 he moved to New York with his older brother Juan Ramón Collazo. During that time, he distinguished himself in the local church in several areas. It is important to point out that during those years in the Spanish barrio he studied for the ministry in a church known today as "La Sinagoga" that was founded by Juan L. Lugo. However, of greatest significance was that he mastered the English language, something that God would use to make him one of the outstanding Christian interpreters of his time. As noted in this book, he served as interpreter for some of the most prominent evangelists of the period.

When Reverend Lugo returned to Puerto Rico to establish the Mizpa Bible Institute in 1937, Antonio Collazo, now 28 years old, also accompanied him to serve as a teacher at the school. Shortly thereafter, he was named Pastor of the First Pentecostal Church in Santurce, and finally, as the National Overseer of the Church of God *Mission Board*. The significance for readers of this volume is to note how Brother Tony's ministerial formation and experience prepared him – both in Puerto Rico and New York City – to eventually establish the Eastern Spanish District of the Church of God east of the Mississippi.

The Puerto Rican economy began to decline in the late 1940s which caused many Church of God pastors to leave there and move to New York City, Chicago, and eventually many other parts of the United States.[1] As the ministry grew, led by Overseer Reverend Henry C. Stoppe and Samuel Irizarry, the pastors felt the need to have a full-time Hispanic Overseer. Most of these pastors had served under the leadership of Antonio Collazo in Puerto Rico, and as a result, at a ministers meeting at the Church of God at 116th Street and Third Avenue, Antonio Collazo was elected Overseer of the Spanish churches east of the Mississippi.

In this, one of Dr. Estrada's best writings, he recounts the sacrificial and successful life of Brother Tony from which we can take many valuable lessons. He accomplishes this by using narratives from his family, friends, and historical data.

Something that you will read later in the book is that following his retirement, Brother Tony enrolled in the New York University system teacher education program at Newburgh, New York. What impressed me most is that he was offered credit for life experience and his previous education, which would have considerably shortened his study at the University, and he chose not to accept. Instead, he chose to follow and the entire complete program. Today he is part of that "great cloud of witnesses"

---

[1] The work of the Church of God east of the Mississippi was initially established primarily by Puerto Ricans, though now it is comprised of virtually all Hispanic nationalities.

Prologue

that encourages us from the galleries of glory to press ahead. Antonio Collazo: A True Apostle!

Dr. Esdras Betancourt

1 August 2017

Introduction

This Project was born when, during a conversation with Pérsida (Tita) Collazo Pagán, one of Reverend Antonio and Persida Lugo Collazo's daughters, where we discussed the possibility of nominating Dr. Collazo for induction in the Hall of the Prophets at the Pentecostal Theological Seminary. We spoke about it with Dr. Kenneth Davis, who was then development Director at the Seminary. He presented the request to the Seminary Board of Trustees where it was approved. Immediately the task of raising the necessary funds to bring the vision to reality was begun. I determined to write a biography of Reverend Collazo as part of the overall design of the project. His widow and children welcomed the proposal with appreciation.

It is important to note that, throughout this book, I have used the more informal term "Brother Tony" when referring to the Reverend Collazo. This in no way implies a diminished view of this giant of the Pentecostal faith among Hispanics and Latinos. On the contrary, it is a term of affection and respect offered by all of us who knew him either closely or from a distance. This was how he referred to himself when approaching his flock and offering them his affection and leadership. It seems to me that this was simply a demonstration of the genuine humility that adorned the excellent ministry of this exceptional man. His consistent and sincere humility were characteristic of his life and service.

In this biography, I have followed the life and ministry of this Apostle to the Hispanic and Latino world in order to discover the personal and ministerial keys that resulted in the successful execution of his ministry. My firm commitment, more than simply lifting up an individual, although certainly warranted in this case, was to find and identify those servant-leader qualities that marked Brother Tony's remarkably successful ministry. If our church leadership, in its developing maturity, can identify his servant-leader qualities and determines to appropriate them today, then I believe I will have accomplished my objective in writing this biography.

I am convinced that beyond those natural qualities that Brother Tony possessed, there were others that he intentionally cultivated and developed to enhance and make his ministry relevant. His passion for reading, education, knowledge of the Biblical text, teaching, preaching, his respect for those he supervised, and many others, were qualities he recognized were necessary for an effective ministry. It is to these servant-leader disciplines that I refer and encourage our current church leadership to cultivate so as to leave a worthy legacy for the generations that follow. This is the best way to pass the baton just as Brother Tony did.

In order to achieve my goal, I have explored several facets of Reverend Antonio Collazo's life and ministry. It has been a wonderfully enriching experience for me, and in the same way, I trust it will be the same for my readers. The journey examining the life and ministry of this Apostle includes several stops which I will explore in each chapter of this work.

The first chapter takes us to the central mountain range of Puerto Rico and to the town of Orocovis. It was in this lovely place that, on May 7, 1910, Manuel Antonio Collazo Rodríguez (Antonio Collazo) was born. He was better known by friends and family simply as "Tony," and later to the church world as "Brother Tony." Here I describe his childhood, conversion to the Pentecostal faith, adolescence and early youth. He moved from the countryside of Orocovis to a similar area near Arecibo, and finally to a poor neighborhood in the city of Santurce.

In the second chapter, we trace his continued migration now to the city of skyscrapers, New York. As was true of many Puerto Ricans during that time, he left with his older brother, Juan Ramón, in search of a *better life.* There he continued his life in the church under the mentorship of Reverend Juan L. Lugo. He also prepared for ministry and married Pérsida Lugo Ortiz, the eldest daughter of Reverend Lugo and his wife Isabelita Ortiz.

Chapter three chronicles Brother Tony's return to Puerto Rico, this time as a professor at Mizpa Bible Institute, known today as Mizpa Pentecostal University. I describe his work as a professor, as associate pastor to Brother Lugo at the Pentecostal Church of God, Inc., located at Calle América in Santurce, and later as pastor of the First Pentecostal Church, Inc., on Calle Europa in Santurce.

Introduction

We continue following the trajectory of Brother Tony's ministry from 1944 to 1958 in chapter four. His service as pastor, along with his wife, Sister Pérsida at the First Pentecostal Church, Inc., and the Church of God *Mission Board* on Calle Europa in Santurce is recounted here.

In chapter five, we take a closer look at his 12-year ministry as Overseer of the Church of God *Mission Board* in Puerto Rico from 1946 until 1958. These are the years when he served as interpreter for United States evangelists T. L. Osborn and Billy Graham. Recounted here are details of the powerful T. L. Osborn crusade in the city of Ponce, Puerto Rico, the emergence of Reverend Antonio Collazo as the undisputed leader of the Pentecostal movement on the Island, and the exponential growth of the Church of God *Mission Board* under his leadership.

A third relocation by the Collazo family, described in chapter six, finds them once again in New York City. He would not return to live in Puerto Rico again. Here we examine his 12 years as Overseer of the Church of God Eastern Spanish District, which encompassed everything east of the Mississippi River with regional offices located in New York City.

The seventh chapter describes Reverend Collazo's service as Overseer of the Spanish churches in the South Central Region of the United States with offices in San Antonio, Texas. This was apparently to be his final ministry assignment as Overseer of the Spanish work in the U.S. prior to his retirement in 1976. However, in 1983, the General Overseer of the Church of God, Dr. Cecil Knight, asked if he would be willing to serve as Overseer of the North Central Spanish District for a year and Brother Tony agreed to this request. This placed Brother Tony and Sister Pérsida, now veteran and experienced leaders, in a different geographic and cultural context than what they had known throughout their ministry.

I invite Reverend Collazo to speak directly to my readers in chapter eight. Here are included several of his articles that were published over a period of years in the Church of God publication *El Evangelio*. I have also included a series of sermon outlines that he edited and that were preserved by his daughter Pérsida (Tita) Collazo Pagán. I am confident that readers will greatly enjoy and appreciate this material.

Chapter nine contains narratives from his wife, son and daughters, relatives, and colleagues in ministry that describe how they viewed Brother Tony. This provides an excellent opportunity to validate those servant-leader qualities he exhibited throughout his ministry. I am of the opinion that these accounts affirm the appropriateness of the title of this biography: *Antonio Collazo: A true Apostle.*

In the final chapter, I relate the account of the departure of the Reverend Antonio Collazo from the fellowship of his own in this temporary kingdom of mortals to enter into the everlasting Kingdom of the eternal God. No doubt, Brother Tony followed the path of all mortals: "Just as people are destined to die once, and after that to face judgment" (Hebrews 9:27 NIV). , however, he will also obtain the reward of all who die in Christ, "so Christ was sacrificed once to take away the sins of many; and he will appear a second time, not to bear sin, but to bring salvation to those who are waiting for him" (Hebrews 9:28 NIV).

Introduction

As is my custom, the book ends with a brief postscript. In this study of the person of Brother Tony, I can reaffirm with certainty that he was a man of special grace, who within his human limitations, maintained his integrity both in his faith and conduct. In the same way, I reemphasize the challenge that we as current leaders face to imitate his faith, and to follow in his footsteps.

However, it is not enough for me to reemphasize the highlights of each chapter. My dear readers, you need to discover the reality of the life and extraordinary ministry of this humble man for yourselves. Reading this work should provide a glimpse into the thoughts, feelings, and actions of this true Apostle of the twentieth century. So, on with your reading!

Chapter 1

Childhood and Early Youth

Nestled in the Central Mountain Range in the heart of Puerto Rico, is the town of Orocovis. It was founded on November 10, 1825 by a group of neighbors led by Juan Prudencio Alvarado, Francisco de Sales Díaz, and Ramón Meléndez. The exact location of the town was in the Barros and Orocovis de Barranquitas district. There was a lady named Eulalia de Rivera, who owned 15 acres of land. She sold 14 and donated the remaining acre for the founding of the town. In the beginning it was named Barros and later Orocovis.

This community is found in the mountainous interior of the Island. It is bounded by Colinda, Ciales, Morovis, and Corozal on the north; Juana Díaz, Villalba, and Coamo to the south; on the west by Ciales, and on the east by Corozal and Barranquitas. Districts or neighborhoods that make up the town include Ala de la Piedra, Barros, Bauta Abajo, Bauta Arriba, Bermejales, Botijas, Cacao, Collores, Damián Abajo,

Childhood and Early Youth

Damián Arriba, Gato, Mata de Cañas, Orocovis, Orocovis Pueblo, Pellejas, Sabana and Saltos. The townspeople are referred to as *orocovenses*. It is also referred to as "the geographic center of Puerto Rico."

It was in this remote area of the Central Mountain range of Puerto Rico that Manuel Antonio Collazo Rodríguez, better known as "Tony" to family and friends; and later as "Hermano Tony" to those in the church world was born on May 7, 1910. After spending his early years in Orocovis, his parents – Juan Antonio Collazo and Carmen Rodríguez – moved to a farm about 15 miles outside the city of Arecibo where they worked in the tobacco fields. It was here where Brother Tony accepted the Lord into his life in 1918, at the tender age of eight. His conversion and that of his family came through the ministry of his maternal uncle Secundino Rodríguez. Interestingly, this uncle who had been a credentialed minister in the Methodist Church near Arecibo, came to know the Pentecostal message through the ministry of Juan L. Lugo, who would later become Brother Tony's father-in-law. Lugo recounted his contact with Secundino as follows:

> In those days there had been a spiritual movement in Arecibo which resulted in the organizing of an evangelical denomination named "Puerto Rican Church." Upon learning of our work in Ponce, Brother Secundino visited us in 1917. We were invited to participate in their first convention where we were represented by Brother Salomón and Brother Panchito. Following the convention, the ministers there decided to place the work, furniture, utensils and all, in the hands of Brother Panchito. He immediately moved to Arecibo to assume

leadership of the church which was located in the Palmarito section of that city.[1]

I include here the following details regarding the conversion experience of Brother Tony, which I published previously.[2]

Henry G. Stoppe, Church of God (Cleveland, TN) missionary on Saint Thomas, published an interesting biographical article in the *Lighted Pathway* in 1945 where he told of the conversion of Reverend Antonio Collazo. This was his account:

His uncle, Secundino Rodríguez, a credentialed minister in the Methodist Church, heard about the arrival of Reverend Juan Lugo from New York as the first Pentecostal missionary to the Island. After attending several of Lugo's services he became convinced beyond a shadow of doubt that this Pentecostal experience was real and for him. He opened his heart to the full Gospel message and with this commitment felt compelled to visit his sister Carmen Rodíguez to share the good news of salvation and of the wonderful Pentecostal experience.

One afternoon in January 1918, Rodríguez along with a group of others from his church came to the

---

[1] Juan L. Lugo, *Pentecostés En Puerto Rico: La Vida de Un Misionero* (San Juan, PR: Puerto Rico Gospel Press, 1951), 52-53.

[2] Wilfredo Estrada-Adorno, *¡Oh poder pentecostal!: Adolescencia temprana madurez e impacto social del pentecostalismo puertorriqueño (1926-1966)*, vol. 3, 100 años después (Trujillo Alto, PR: Ediciones Guardarraya, 2017).

farm where Tony Collazo lived with his parents. His father, Juan Antonio Collazo sent his two boys, Tony and Ramón, out on horseback to invite his neighbors to come to his house that evening to attend a religious service.

The next morning Tony's parents, Juan Antonio Collazo and Carmen Rodríguez, Tony, his older brother (Juan Ramón Collazo Rodríguez), his older sister (Ramona del Carmen Collazo Rodríguez), and his two uncles were baptized in water. After the baptismal service, the congregation followed Tony's father to the warehouse where his tobacco harvest was drying. In the blink of an eye he took it out to the road in front of the congregation and set the entire crop, which represented his harvest for that year, afire. From that point going forward Juan Antonio Collazo never again harvested tobacco.[3]

Brother Tony's immediate family included his parents Juan Antonio Collazo and Carmen Rodríguez and the following siblings: Ramona del Carmen Torres, born on September 16, 1904, Juan Ramón Collazo Rodríguez[4], born March 22, 1906, Manuel Antonio Collazo Rodríguez (Brother Tony), born May 7, 1910, María Victoria Pérez, born December 10, 1913, Isabel Cristina Acevedo, born

---

[3] Henry G. Stoppe, "A Short Biography of Brother Collazo: Missionary and Assistant Overseer of Puerto Rico," *The Lighted Pathway*, October 1945, 10, quoted by Estrada-Adorno, *¡Oh poder pentecostal!*, 3:132.

[4] Juan Ramón Collazo Rodríguez was the father of Reverend Loida Collazo Camacho, wife of Reverend Héctor Camacho Hernández.

April 1, 1915, Carmen María Pérez[5], born December 10, 1917, and Celia Colón, paternal half-sister, born September 11, 1945.[6]

As was previously mentioned, Secundino Rodríguez was instrumental in leading the entire Collazo-Rodríguez family to accept the Pentecostal message. The initial contact between Brother Secundino and Juan L. Lugo established a relationship between the Collazo and Lugo families that would be nurtured in the Pentecostal Church of God, Inc. of the General Council of the Assemblies of God in Santurce. It continued through the years in the church "La Sinagoga" in the Puerto Rican Barrio of New York City, and finally at the Church of God at Third Avenue and 116th Street in Manhattan.

The early childhood and adolescent experiences of Brother Tony at the Pentecostal Church of God in Santurce contributed to his spiritual formation and leadership development under the tutelage first of missionary Lena S. Howe and later under the mentorship of Juan Lugo, who some years later would become his father-in-law. It was in this church where he actively participated in the youth services clearly demonstrating his unmistakable leadership qualities.

During the time of the family's relationship with the Pentecostal Church of God in Santurce, the horrible

---

[5] Carmen María Pérez was the wife of Johnny Pérez, an outstanding pupil of Juan L. Lugo.

[6] This family information was provided by Raquel Collazo Lugo, daughter of Antonio and Pérsida Collazo

effects of the Great Depression that gripped the United States loomed darkly over Puerto Rico along with the devastating effects of the San Felipe the Second hurricane of 1928. From an economic and social standpoint, the Great Depression affected the lives of the entire Puerto Rican populace. As was to be expected, those living on the fringes of society suffered more than the general population. Additionally, the hurricane, with 160 mph winds as it passed over the Island caused widespread destruction estimated at more than $50M and resulted in the deaths of 312 persons. A cloud of desperation enveloped the Island.[7]

Faced with a reality of hopelessness and anxiety on the Island in the late 1920s and early 1930s, the two brothers, Antonio and Ramón immigrated to New York City in search of a better life. We will find them in the city of skyscrapers in the next chapter. So then let us move on up North with Brother Tony!

---

[7] Estrada-Adorno, ¡Oh poder pentecostal!, 3:51.

Chapter 2

Seeking a Better Tomorrow in the City of Skyscrapers

During the social and economic catastrophe of the 1930s, the emigration from Puerto Rico continued to the cities of the eastern United States, and especially to New York City. There, in what came to be known as the "Barrio," or Spanish Harlem bounded by 96th Street on the south, 125th Street on the north, 5th Avenue on the west, and the East River on the east, is where most Puerto Ricans settled from the 1920s forward. A small group of Pentecostals, most who came from the Barrio, started a church in the Greenpoint area of Brooklyn.

The Pentecostal Church of God, Inc. sent Tomás Álvarez to pastor them in 1929. At their Convention in 1931, Brother Álvarez reported on the strong development of that church, however, he did not return to New York. Reverend Juan L. Lugo left Puerto Rico in March of that year to assume the pastorate of the Greenpoint congregation. After a month he returned to the Island to bring his entire family, and, in April 1931 he settled in as the pastor. He left a fruitful 15 years of ministry behind as the pioneer Pentecostal missionary to Puerto Rico.[1]

In October 1931 Brother Lugo started a Pentecostal Church of God work on 104th Street in Spanish Harlem because he recognized that much of the Puerto Rican immigration during that time was not centered in Brooklyn, but in East Harlem. Consequently, he undertook the task of

Current location of "La Sinagoga" at 125th Street and Park Avenue in "El Barrio", NYC.

starting this church in tandem with the Greenpoint congregation in Brooklyn. Lugo's oldest daughter, Pérsida Lugo Collazo remembers that the building "was large, clean, and pretty."[2] Brother Lugo did not leave the Greenpoint church but simply added a new missionary endeavor to his ministerial work. The miraculous and rapid growth of this new congregation resulted in them outgrowing the facility on 104th Street by June 1932. Brother Lugo took a prodigious step of faith on June 17th and moved the church to a building that became known as "La Sinagoga" on 109th Street between Park and

---

[1] Lugo, *Pentecostés En Puerto Rico*, 95–96.

[2] Personal interview by the author with Sister Pérsida at her daughter Raquel's home in Saint Petersburg, FL on May 19, 2017. Also present were her daughters Ligia and Raquel, her son Juan Antonio (Totoño), and the author's wife Carmen.

Madison Avenues in the heart of the "Barrio."[3] The rapid growth of this church intensified the workload to the point that Brother Lugo handed over the pastorate of the Greenpoint church to other ministers in 1933.[4]

Antonio (Tony) Collazo

Wedding photo of Tony and Persis in November 1936

These developments helped pave the way for Brother Tony to reconnect with his Pastor from Santurce in New York City. Both Tony and his older brother Ramón had emigrated to the City in search of a better life in 1929 in an effort to escape the disastrous economic situation on the in Puerto Rico. While in Santurce he had received his initial training as a youth leader under the pastoral mentorship of Brother Lugo. Now they meet again in this city of skyscrapers as part of the Puerto Rican diaspora. For nearly a decade Brother Tony sat under the watchful pastoral eye of this giant of the Pentecostal faith.

Brother Tony joined the Pentecostal church in New York that Brother Lugo – the pioneer Pentecostal missionary to

---

[3] As a result of Urban Development in the City in 1959, "La Sinagoga" relocated to 125th Street and Park Avenue. The church retains the iconic name "La Sinagoga" and it remains to this day as an indelible witness as one of the most impactful Pentecostal churches in Spanish Harlem.

[4] Lugo, *Pentecostés En Puerto Rico*, 97.

Puerto Rico – later came to pastor. There he received additional Christian formation training and quickly assumed a leadership role in the church. He faithfully served for several years in highly responsible roles as deacon, youth leader, Sunday School superintendent, and leader of the open air services.[5] Interestingly his relationship with Brother Lugo would eventually become much closer as he married Lugo's oldest daughter Pérsida on November 27, 1936. When they married she was 17 and he was 26 years old.

Pérsida was born April 13, 1919 in Ponce, Puerto Rico the oldest of six children. Her siblings were Benjamín, John Jr., Elizabeth, Abigail, and Hulda. Children born to Tony and Pérsida were Ligia Isabel, Juan Antonio, Pérsida, Raquel and Rebecca. She faithfully supported Brother

Tony throughout his ministry. This ideal partnership occasionally demanded great personal and family sacrifice, but she continued on following the path that the Lord had assigned to them both. There were times when she had to leave an ideal house to squeeze into a small apartment, but she willingly did so because of the immense satisfaction

Pérsida Lugo Collazo

---

[5] Stoppe, "A Short Biography of Brother Collazo: Missionary and Assistant Overseer of Puerto Rico," October 1945, 10. See Esdras Betancourt, *En el espíritu y poder de pentecostés: Historia de la iglesia de Dios hispana en Estados Unidos* (Cleveland, TN: CEL Publicaciones, 2016).

derived from sharing in ministry with her husband.

As the daughter of the pioneer Pentecostal missionary couple to Puerto Rico, and later to the eastern United States, Pérsida had first-hand knowledge of the sometimes harsh realities and limitations imposed upon a family in ministry. Most of the time, because she was the oldest child, when her parents were away from the family attending to their ministerial duties, she was left in charge of her younger brothers and sisters. Consequently, she had no desire to marry a minister. On the one hand, truth is that she did not marry a minister. When they married Tony worked as a supervisor in a mattress factory in New York.

On the other hand, even while working in that mattress factory, for seven years Brother Tony served in the local church under the close guidance of Brother Lugo. During that time, he studied at the Assembly of God Bible Institute in the City from which he graduated in 1936. All of this preparation began to prepare the way for his first missionary assignment. In a marvelous work of grace, the Lord was already preparing Brother Lugo's heart to return to Puerto Rico to, among other responsibilities, establish a Bible Institute. With that calling in mind, he began the task of preparing those young people in New York who would accompany him on what would become his final trip to the Island on appointment by the General Council of the Assemblies of God. That group included Brother

Tony, Johnny Pérez,[6] and Julia Camacho.[7] Additionally, Sister Isabelita Lugo would also serve as one of the teachers in this endeavor.

In the summer of 1936 the Lugo family made a trip to San Jose, California to visit his mother, Sister Juana and his sister Carmela. After spending two months with the family they returned by way of Springfield, Missouri where they visited the International Offices of the Assemblies of God. While there he received instructions to return to Puerto Rico and establish a Bible Institute. Before leaving on this trip, Pérsida had become engaged to Brother Tony and had expressed her desire to drop the school venture. She recounts how he said to her: "If you abandon the school project, then we are getting married." On the return from California, her account continues: "We made the

---

[6] Juan Pérez Hernandez, better known as Johnny Pérez was one of many "adopted" children of Reverend Juan and Isabelita Lugo. He married Carmen (Melín) Collazo Rodríguez who was Brother Tony's sister.

[7] Julia Camacho, later known by her married name Julia Valentine, was the daughter of Ramón and Nicolasa Camacho who were part of the Puerto Rican group that organized a small church in Danville the San Francisco Bay area of California around 1917. They had returned from Hawaii to work in the agricultural fields around the Bay. Among those in that group were Francisco Ortiz, Sr., Ángelo Fraticelli, Domingo Cruz, and Ramón and Nicolasa Camacho. This pair, along with others, was baptized in water following an evangelistic meeting with Evangelist Francisco Olazábel in 1917. See: Víctor De León, *The Silent Pentecostals: A Biographical History of the Pentecostal Movement among the Hispanics in the Twentieth Century* (Taylor, SC: Faith Printing Company, 1979), 27.

necessary plans and were married on November 27 of that year (1936)."[8]

It was on January 11, 1937 that Brother Lugo left for Puerto Rico with his family and the young lady Julia Camacho, who would discharge various responsibilities in the Bible Institute. His oldest daughter, Pérsida, had married Antonio Collazo the previous November and remained behind. Reflecting on this experience said: "Although we felt a degree of sadness leaving our daughter, we thanked the Lord that he had provided a true servant of God."[9] Lugo and his group arrived in San Juan on January 13, 1937, which preceded by one year the return of Brother Tony and Pérsida to join in ministry at the Bible Institute and at the Pentecostal Church of God in Santurce.

We will review Brother Tony's ministry alongside Reverend Lugo in Puerto Rico over a three-year period in the next chapter. Let us then continue following the trajectory of ministry of this young leader of the church. Join me as we turn the page!

---

[8] Lugo Collazo interview on May 19, 2017. Also present were her daughters Ligia and Raquel, her son Juan Antonio (Totoño), and the author's wife Carmen.

[9] Lugo, *Pentecostés En Puerto Rico*, 107.

Chapter 3

Returning to Puerto Rico along with his mentor and

father-in-law Juan L. Lugo

After having returned to Puerto Rico on January 13, 1937, Brother Lugo immediately plunged into three new responsibilities on the Island. He supervised the Pentecostal Church of God, Inc. that was affiliated with the General Council of the Assemblies of God, pastored the local Santurce congregation of that denomination, and set about establishing and directing the Mizpa Bible Institute. His notes regarding his return to Puerto Rico are as follows:

We arrived at our beloved land on January 13, 1937. There to meet us was our dear brother Andrés Rodríguez, pastor of the Pentecostal church in Santurce who was accompanied by some of his congregation. That same evening this wonderful group from the church extended a warm welcome to us.

We settled in Santurce and began to visit the churches across the Island until time for the Annual Assemblies of God Conference for the District of Puerto Rico. There they elected me as Superintendent.

That summer, the pastor of the church in Ponce, Brother Luis C. Otero and his wife left for Chile by way of New York. They received a heartfelt farewell from all and prayers for a fruitful ministry in the field to which, according to their testimony, the Lord had called them. With the Ponce pulpit now vacant, Brother Rodríguez asked to be transferred there.

I then assumed pastorate of the Santurce congregation which, according to the report presented some months earlier at the Conference consisted of 411 members. By September I had visited most of the churches across the Island and subsequently began to prepare for the opening of the Bible Institute.

Brother Juan Pérez Hernández, who we warmly referred to as Johnny, arrived from New York. He would translate the curriculum materials from English into Spanish and properly format them for the students. He immediately began the arduous task, and with the Lord's help we opened the "Mizpa" Bible Institute in September 1937 with 16 students from various towns. I served as Director, while my wife and Brother Pérez taught the classes, and Sister Camacho was the Dean of Students.[1]

The initial year at the Institute was launched with this cadre of four forming the leadership team. During the Christmas break of 1937 Sister Pérsida came to Puerto Rico to visit her parents. She told her mother that she was pregnant and recalls her reply: "My daughter, I am too

---

[1] Ibid., 109-110.

busy with the work of the Bible Institute to return to New York to be with you during this time. If you stay here, I will be able to help." Sister Pérsida also remembered her conversation with her husband: "I talked with Tony and he encouraged me to remain in Puerto Rico while he worked a while longer in New York in order to save some money and join her a little later on the Island."[2] So she remained with her parents and stayed in a small house at the back of the church on America Street in Santurce.

I must mention as a sad historical note that, even as her mother greatly desired to be with her during this pregnancy, Pérsida lost that first child. Her son Manuel Antonio Collazo Lugo was strangled by a tangled umbilical cord. Pérsida recounted: "The midwife did not get there in time. When she arrived, the child was already dead as he had strangled on the umbilical cord."[3]

As we can see, it is difficult to explain how missionaries, so completely dedicated to the Lord's service, were not exempt from such difficult and complicated trials. In the world of theological study, we associate these kinds of challenges with the term *theodicy.* This theological discipline seeks to explain the goodness and justice of God in view of the existence of suffering and evil in the world. Without a doubt, the child being stillborn has to have shaken this family that had left the stability of New York to come and serve in their native country in the face of

---

[2] Lugo Collazo interview on May 19, 2017. Personal interview conducted by the author at her daughter's home in Saint Petersburg, FL.

[3] Ibid.

such challenging social and economic circumstances. Now their first son is stillborn. I am certain that understanding the pain caused by the death of their child in the face of a loving and omnipotent God was very difficult for Tony and Pérsida. However, their faith in a sovereign God served to strengthen and encourage them so that they did not feel compelled to have to explain or defend Him. Their trust in God allowed them to move forward in their life and ministry where they proclaimed the supernatural intervention of God in the daily life of the people in spite of their own deep personal loss.

At the end of the first year of classes at the Mizpa Bible Institute, Brother Lugo traveled to New York to raise funds for the continued operation of the school. In addition to that goal, he sought to convince his son-in-law, Tony Collazo, whose wife was already in Puerto Rico, to come and join the faculty at Mizpa. While Lugo continued fundraising in New York, Tony traveled to the Island to join his wife and to become part of the faculty. This trip, toward the end of 1938, signaled the start of a very successful and greatly satisfying ministry for this missionary couple. Brother Lugo wrote in his memoirs: "Upon my return to the Island we began the second year of our religious training effort and Brother Collazo assumed the Bible Chair."[4] At the time that he joined the faculty, Brother Tony was barely 28 years old. This young minister had worked closely under the tutelage of Brother Lugo in New York and had distinguished himself as an excellent teacher.

---

[4] Lugo, *Pentecostés En Puerto Rico,*

When Brother Lugo returned from his fundraising mission on behalf of the Mizpa Bible Institute to finance the second year of study, he had a second ministerial responsibility for Brother Tony to assume. It happened that the church in Santurce was growing at a dizzying pace, and, although they had expanded the sanctuary, it could not hold the crowds. Since the church had a satellite location in the Sunoco sector of Santurce, Brother Lugo decided to establish that location as a separate church from the main body. Since Brother Johnny Pérez, in addition to serving on the faculty of the Bible Institute, also served as Brother Lugo's Assistant Pastor, he was assigned as pastor of the new work at Sunoco. In order to fill the pastoral vacancy at the Santurce location, Brother Tony was installed as the Assistant Pastor.[5] This marked the second phase in the ministry of Brother and Sister Collazo. From that time until 1958 they would be associated with the pastoral ministry in Santurce.

In 1940 the Reverend Manuel Antonio Collazo Rodríguez[6] was ordained to the ministry in the Pentecostal Church of God of the General Council of the Assemblies of God by Reverend Manuel T. Sánchez. That same year, along with Reverend Lugo, he withdrew from fellowship with the Pentecostal Church of God and returned to New

---

[5] Ibid.

[6] Brother Tony thought that his given name was Manuel Antonio Collazo Rodríguez until later in his life, when he discovered that his Baptismal Certificate identified him simply as Antonio Collazo Rodríguez. His only copy of the document is included in the attachments of this work.

York with his family. In my book *¡Oh poder pentecostal!: Adolescencia, temprana madurez e impacto social del pentecostalismo (1926-1966)*, I note the following regarding his return to Puerto Rico:

> Antonio Collazo returned to Puerto Rico in 1941 to pastor the First Pentecostal Church, Inc. This congregation emerged as a result of the strong differences between the leaders of the local Pentecostal Church of God church in Santurce and their denominational authorities. These disagreements resulted in the departure of Brother Lugo as pastor in 1940 and the naming of Fabricano Picón to succeed him. After a time, the denominational leaders wanted to replace him with Benigno Rodríguez Colón, the Secretary of the denomination. There was strong opposition to this move from the local church leadership which resulted in a lawsuit in which the Pentecostal Church of God, Inc. prevailed.[7] The group that supported Pastor Picón withdrew from the church in Santurce and organized as the First Pentecostal Church. This is the congregation that Reverend Antonio Collazo came to serve in 1941. He pastored the newly named church until October 1945 when he, along with four other churches and their pastors under his oversight united with the Church of God *Mission*

---

[7] Helen Santiago provides a detailed account of this in her book: Helen Santiago, *El pentecostalismo de Puerto Rico: Al compás de una fe autóctona (1916-1956)* (Trujillo Alto, PR: Helen Santiago, 2015), 207–210. Helen Santiago, *El pentecostalismo de Puerto Rico: Al compás de una fe autóctona (1916-1956)* (Trujillo Alto, PR: Helen Santiago, 2015), 207–210.

Board, which had begun its work in Puerto Rico in 1944.[8]

From the time Brother Tony affiliated with the Church of God *M.B.* in their first convention conducted at the church located at the Parada $16^{1/2}$ in Santurce pastored by Reverend Lorenzo Balcasa Delgado, he "became the catalyst that energized the organization in its first years of life."[9] The churches that came into the new denomination at that time were the following: (1) Barrio Hoare in Santurce pastored by Tomás de Jesus, (2) Villa Palmera, Santurce, pastored by Juan Falero, (3) Corozal, pastored by Nicomeded Valcárcel, (4) Barrio Ingenio in Toa Baja, pastored by Saturnino Rodríguez, and (5) First Church of God, Santurce pastored by Antonio Collazo[10]

Carl J. Hughes and wife

The Church of God (Cleveland, TN) ordained Manuel A. Collazo (Brother Tony) on December 11, 1945. Officiating at the ordination service was Reverend Carl. J Hughes who was the first Church of God Superintendent of the West Indies. In this way, his credentials as an ordained minister were immediately accepted when he united with the Church of God. On December 31, 1945, the Church of God

---

[8] Estrada-Adorno, *¡Oh poder pentecostal!*, 3:117.

[9] Miguel Navas, *Compendio de Minutas de La Iglesia de Dios "M. B." de Puerto Rico* (Saint Just, PR, 1969), 11.

[10] Ibid.

Mission Board asked Reverend C. E. French to move to the Dominican Republic to oversee ministry in that country. At that point Reverend Collazo became his assistant charged with oversight of the work in Puerto Rico. Later Reverend Hughes followed Brother French when he left for India as missionary, and Brother Tony became his assistant.

The Church of God at the Parada 22 in Santurce became the hub of ministry outreach for the Church of God *Mission Board* (hereafter *M. B.*) in Puerto Rico. We will follow the warm and loving pastoral ministry of Reverend Collazo in the next chapter. So then, let us move on!

Chapter 4

Antonio Collazo: Pastor of the Church of God Mission Board at Parada 22 in Santurce

The pastoral life at the church at Parada 22 was exciting and one of heavy responsibility for the Collazo-Lugo family. All of their children – Ligia, Juan Antonio, Pérsida, Raquel, and Rebecca – were already born when they joined the Church of God. This family was well loved, very involved with the community, and, with a high level of personal commitment, fully confident in God's supernatural intervention in the daily lives of the people.

Collazo family, Christmas 1958

There are many accounts of this daily supernatural intervention of God in individual lives and in the weekly worship services. Some years later, at a convention of the North Central Spanish Region in 1983, I personally had occasion to hear Brother Tony recount one of those instances of divine interruption that changed the life of the church and of the people.[1] He

---

[1] After his retirement in 1976, in 1983 then General Overseer of the Church of God Dr. Cecil Knight asked Brother Tony to serve for a

remembered the powerful prayer services of the church at Parada 22 held on Thursday mornings with a large number of ladies. There was a sister in the faith that lived near the church with a son who suffered from a mental illness. He was so aggressive because of the illness that he had to be kept in a locked cage in the lower level of the house. Brother Tony recounted that on one Thursday morning after the prayer service he and the ladies who had been praying decided to visit the home where this sick youth lived.

When they arrived, he told the mother: "We have prayed for your son in our meeting this morning at the church, and we feel that the Lord has sent us to your house to personally pray for your son because He will heal him today." Immediately she showed Brother Tony the cage where her son was kept. Brother Tony asked for the key, so he could unlock it and go inside to pray for the young man. His mother responded to her pastor: "No pastor, the boy is very aggressive and could hurt you." Upon his insistence, she reluctantly gave him the key and Brother Tony unlocked the door and went in while the ladies earnestly prayed at the top of their voices. He put his hands on the youth and confidently prayed for a miracle from God to heal him. After the prayer, he closed the door of the cage, gave the keys back to the mother, and left the house along with the group of ladies.

---

year as interim Overseer of the North Central Spanish Region until a new Overseer could be named. He graciously accepted for that year and served the church in this time of need.

Brother Tony continued the account. On the following Sunday evening service which was full to overflowing, during the time for testimonies, he asked if anyone wanted to share anything about the miraculous intervention of God in their lives that week. Suddenly, from the back of the church, a young man stood up and said: "I want to testify" as he moved toward the altar. When he reached the front, he said: "But I want to testify with a song" as he reached for the microphone. Although Brother Tony managed to hang onto it the young man began to testify with words similar to these:

I wandered through this world without faith, without hope

Not knowing that there was a Savior

Who in order to save my soul from death

Came into the world and died for me on a cross

I am happy, yes I am happy

Since Christ has redeemed me

I am happy, yes I am happy

Since Christ has redeemed me

You were the lily that perfumed my soul

Giving me the joy that I could not find in the world

You delivered me from condemnation

And today I testify of my glorious salvation

When in this life I find myself saddened

I call on you my wonderful Savior

Praying that you will comfort my soul

So that I can overcome the world, Lord

Close, very close to you is where I want to be

To feel the grace of your divine love

Because without you, life is bitter

You are the fount of my consolation

You sinner, who lives without hope

Look to Calvary where Jesus died

There he took your failures and sins

To give you life and eternal salvation

This hymn[2] was written by a young man who was miraculously healed by God through the ministry of a pastor and church that believed in the supernatural power of God. His name was Goyito Montalvo. He became a strong Christian, hymn writer, and powerful witness to the community as to the amazing power of God in the lives of his people. Many Christian artists have sung and recorded this hymn titled "My Testimony", but I doubt if they fully understood the miraculous back story of a "wrapping paper" composer, as he was called by José Joaquín (Tato)

---

[2] The original text of this composition, although other versions have developed over time, was provided by Sister Dora Hilda Colón, member of the Church of God *M.B.* in Pugnado, Manatí. Her pastor, Tato Guadalupe sent me the copy that is included in the attachments of this book.

Guadalupe.³ He used that reference to the writers because whenever the inspiration that came from above hit them, they grabbed the first piece of paper they found to write the thought or idea down. His poems, written from a personal experience of encounter with the incarnate God, as is true of this song, have passed from generation

to generation as irrefutable evidence of the power and grace of God who found him and transformed his life of hopelessness and despair into a new life full of many possibilities.

Brother Tony, along with some members, in front of the church at Parada 22.

Testimonies about the miraculous intervention of God in the lives of the church members as well as those in the larger community were constantly being shared as part of the Pentecostal services. This was the "daily bread" in those worship experiences. As a result, the ministry of this pastor-teacher saturated the lives of that community in Santurce as well as the surrounding neighborhoods touched by the outreach of the Church of God *M.B. T*he distinction as pastor-teacher ascribed to Brother Tony, refined during his educational ministry at Mizpa Bible Institute, remained throughout the entirety of his long ministry. Antonino Bonilla describes his extraordinary pastoral work in this

---

³ Tato Guadalupe is an exquisite singer and musician, pastor of the Church of God *M.B.* in the Pugnado section of Manatí. He is the son of the late minister of our church Joaquín Guadalupe, and my adopted son.

way: "His manner of pastoral leadership was very effective. He transformed the Church of God at the Parada 22 into a city of refuge for those who passed by and also for the many that were actually integrated into the life of the church."[4]

Another of his gifted students, Manuel Pérez Sánchez, tells of an instance that occurred early in his life while Brother Tony pastored the church at Parada 22 in Santurce.

I was passing by Brother Tony's office one day when he invited me to approach his desk. He said, "I have two sacks of chicken feathers and I want you to go to the El Nilo[5] bakery. Once you get there begin to spread the feathers out along Europa Street coming back toward the church. Then I want you to retrace your steps and pick up every feather without missing a one." Pérez Sánchez responded: "That is impossible Brother Tony," to which he responded: "Always remember the following; when the character of a minister is impugned, even if it is a lie, some people will believe it and it becomes virtually impossible to repair the damage done. Guard

---

[4] Antonino Bonilla, interview by Wilfredo Estrada-Adorno, June 4, 2017.

[5] The El Nilo bakery and cake shop was located on Ponce de Leon Avenue in Santurce near the Central High School. Brother Tony's office was located at the Church of God on Europa Street, about a ten minute walk from the bakery.

yourself from getting into a situation that would harm the character of a fellow minister."[6]

Brother Pérez Sánchez affirms that this lesson, from early in his Christian formation, has remained with him throughout his entire Christian life. Without a doubt, Brother Tony's exceptional pastoral care for the youth who sat under his instruction impacted their ministry in significant ways. It is important to note that his influential ministry was largely formulated as pastor of the Church of God *M.B.* on Europa Street in Santurce, which was generally referred to as Parada 22. His pastoral work in that church evolved into a vital link in the Pentecostal movement of that city. Since 1945 this church, under the pastoral direction of Brother Tony and Sister Pérsida, has become the iconic expression of the Church of God *M.B.* in Puerto Rico. It became the engine that propelled the outreach of this relatively new denominational endeavor. Many conventions, ministers meetings along with the denominational offices for the Island were located there. It also served as the first home of the Bible Institute that is known today as the Theological University of the Caribbean.

Another important aspect of Brother Tony's ministry in Puerto Rico was his work as interpreter for the well-known evangelists who came to the Island. Among others, he served as interpreter for Tommy Lee (T.L.) Osborn, Billy Graham, and Oral Roberts. He stood alongside Billy Graham at his massive rallies that attracted throngs of people.

---

[6] Telephone interview with Reverend Maunel Pérez Sánchez conducted by Wilfredo Estrada Adorno, May 9, 2017.

In the same way, he was there with T.L. Osborn in the decade of the 1950s at the powerful healing campaigns that impacted all of Puerto Rico. One such meeting in Ponce attracted many sick people seeking help, including paralytics, the lame, blind, and those suffering from tuberculosis. Miraculous healings occurred by the hand of God through the ministry of this preacher from Oklahoma and his interpreter Antonio Collazo.

Brother Tony also served as interpreter in the healing ministry of evangelist Oral Roberts. His expertise in interpreting from English to Spanish was highly regarded by organizers of the evangelistic campaigns of ministers from the United States. He was always their first choice to minister along with the evangelists who came to the Island. Clearly, his service in this capacity to world-renowned evangelists afforded him an influential place of honor among the Pentecostal leaders of the period in Puerto Rico.

Coming up in the next chapter, we will explore more fully Reverend Collazo's role as Overseer of the Church of God *Mission Board* for a period of twelve years from 1946 until 1958. During this time the Pentecostal church on the Island was led by a man who was truly out of the ordinary. So, join me as we explore his work in this amazing world!

Chapter 5

Antonio Collazo:
Overseer of the Church of God *Mission Board*

Henry G. Stoppe and wife

Concurrent with his pastorate of the church at Parada 22, starting in 1946 Reverend Collazo also served as Overseer of the Church of God *M.B.* under the supervision of Carl J. Hughes, Superintendent of the West Indies from 1945 to 1950. His work during this period resulted in significant results. Brother Tony continued his work under the supervision of Reverend Henry G. Stoppe who succeeded Reverend Hughes from 1950 to 1954 and the church continued to grow at an almost dizzying pace. From 1954 to 1958 he served under the direction of Reverend Aaron W. Brummett who actually served as Superintendent of the West Indies until 1962.

Describing his experience as Superintendent of the Church of God *M.B.*, Reverend Henry C. Stoppe wrote the following in 1946:

When Brother French was named Overseer of the work on the Island, Brother Collazo extended him warm friendship and cooperation. After more than a year of collaboration, during which he familiarized himself with the teachings and polity of the Church of God, he decided to join us. This past October of 1945, Brother Collazo and his church (First Pentecostal Church) along with another five congregations and their pastors whom he supervised also united with the Church of God. Some months later he was named Assistant Superintendent. Since that time, he has worked faithfully to promote the ministry of the church through all means available. The church on the Island has experienced significant progress in the past year. We now have 20 churches and several missions.[1]

Clearly the growth mentioned above was exponential. In 1944 the Church of God *M.B.* had begun with four

A.W.
Brummett

churches. The twenty churches and various missions in 1946 were evidence of the hard and effective work of Brothers Collazo and Hughes. Later Brother Stoppe became Brother Tony's supervisor when he assumed leadership of the Church of God in the West Indies from 1950-1954. When Brother Tony left Puerto Rico for New York in 1958 to assume leadership of the Spanish churches

---

[1] Stoppe, "A Short Biography of Brother Collazo: Missionary and Assistant Overseer of Puerto Rico," October 1945, 10.

east of the Mississippi, the ministry had grown from 4 to 65 churches and several missions. Without a doubt the growth during this period was very rapid. God gave the increase while employing the gifts and leadership of Brother Tony. The work of God in the world is always accompanied by the unquestioning response and dedication of those called by God. Reverend Antonio Collazo did his part in God's divine endeavor with the development of Church of God in Puerto Rico during his tenure as Overseer.

In addition to his splendid evangelistic and missionary work, Brother Tony also organized a Bible Institute that was located upstairs in his church facility at Parada 22. It was started in 1956 with six students who also lodged at the church. In this way, much like his own pastor and father-in-law Reverend Juan L. Lugo, he effectively combined the evangelistic and missionary outreach with academics. He never acknowledged any separation between Pentecostal spirituality and formal preparation for the ministry. For that reason, he sent many ministerial candidates to study in the Bible Institutes and seminaries of the church.

The arduous work of Brother Collazo as Assistant Superintendent of the Church of God in Puerto Rico yielded immediate and significant results. Writing about this growth in October of 1946, Brother C.E. French said:

We were pleased to find the work prospering and growing. Our precious Brother Collazo had given much of his time to get our itinerary prepared so that we could cover most of our work in the short time that we had before the convention. Brother Hughes joined us after his visit in Saint Thomas. We went into some new fields and opened the work for the Church. We approved some new projects, and deeded some new church buildings to the Church, as well as receiving the entire membership. Only by visiting Puerto Rico can one get a real view of the Church's progress and an appreciation of the work that those precious men are doing for the Church of God.

The convention opened on schedule with the power and presence of God to see us through. Many good sermons were given by our local men, sermons with power and spirituality, sermons that American preachers could appreciate and enjoy. Every one of our brethren worked faithfully to see his part of the convention a success. Although it ran into hundreds of dollars and required much work, our brethren paid the way and had money to spare at its closing. [2]

From early in his ministry Reverend Collazo demonstrated an affable and caring character that was recognized by his colleagues and supervisors. In particular they noted his gentle and kind treatment of pastors and church members under his supervision. These qualities resulted in him being loved by all. Once again, Brother French commented about his outstanding leadership qualities.

Brother Antonio Collazo, who is now acting as assistant supervisor to Brother Carl J. Hughes, is certainly proving himself a great man of wisdom and ability. He understands his own people and has a spirit of LOVE

---

[2] "C. E. and Helen French," *The Church of God Evangel*, October 12, 1946, 6–7.

and CONSIDERATION that gets him into the homes and hearts of the people. His work of the past speaks for him. He suffered for some time as a local pastor in a small church, but today he has the largest Pentecostal church in the entire Island; and since Pentecost is the leading Protestant movement down there, he has the leading church among them all.[3]

It was these qualities that helped Brother Tony develop his congregation at Parada 22 as a growing and influential church during his time as pastor through 1958. From there he left for New York City to become the Overseer of the Eastern Spanish District of the Church of God. This area encompassed the entire country east of the Mississippi River.

The growth of the church in Puerto Rico continued in large part because of the leadership of Brother Tony. Initially his support of missionaries French and Hughes as their assistant, and later as the Overseer himself, God prospered the work. By 1946 the church numbered 22 congregations with 1364 members. There was a contagious spiritual fervor that resulted in many conversions and baptisms in the Holy Spirit. Revival had descended upon this new Pentecostal movement on the Island in a miraculous way.

Using his administrative gifts, Brother Tony provided organizational structure to the fledgling Pentecostal church so that it could continue its orderly growth. His absolute commitment to develop a well prepared

---

[3] Ibid.

Pentecostal community early in his tenure (1950) led him to establish the Sunday School department under the direction of experienced pastor Fabricano Picón. This pastor had been nurtured under the tutelage of Juan L. Lugo in New York and had spent over a decade pastoring on the Island. Continuing the same vision of developing a church that would serve the needs of different generations he organized the Youth department in 1951. It was led by Ángel Berganzo who was one of the four pastors who united with the Church of God *M.B.* in 1944. He assumed his duties as denominational Youth director which were added to his responsibilities as pastor of the church at Coto Norte de Manatí.

An extraordinary circumstance placed Reverend Collazo right in the middle of one of the most impressive evangelistic campaigns ever to occur on the Island. I refer to the previously mentioned visit of American evangelist T.L. Osborn, who was not well known at the time, and his wife Daisy. The campaign was held in Ponce. Osborn and his wife had just returned from a "disappointing experience as missionaries to India."[4]

Following that painful experience in India, Osborn dedicated himself to ministry as an evangelist. He and his wife left for an evangelistic crusade in Jamaica. There he encountered Church of God missionary Henry Stoppe who discussed the possibility of evangelist Osborn visiting Puerto Rico. He later discussed Osborn's evangelistic ministry with Reverend Collazo considering the possibility of

---

[4] T. L. Osborn, *Personal Diary Notes: The Ponce, Puerto Rico Crusade and Its Significance* (Ladonna Osborn, 2007), 3.

such a visit. Immediately, Brother Tony and the missionary from the Foursquare Church, Norman Smith joined forces to bring T.L. Osborn to Ponce in 1950. They planned to hold the meeting in the baseball stadium, but the Mayor, Andrés Grillasca Salas, denied their request. In light of his refusal to allow use of the baseball stadium they secured the theater La Perla with a seating capacity of 1500. Osborn made this observation in his diary about the first service: "Fifty four people accepted Christ in the first service. Daisy and I prayed for six people who were instantaneously healed, and the audience realized that God was in their midst."[5] Subsequent to the miracles on that first night, what followed was the start of a revival throughout the entire city. Osborn continued to record in his diary as follows:

> The second day the theater was full and 126 received Christ. We prayed for the daughter of the Chief of Police who, when she was helped to the platform, could barely walk with her two crutches. But she laid the crutches aside and came down from the platform walking perfectly. Other amazing miracles occurred that night.[6]

Truly great things began to happen from the third night forward. That night the people could no longer fit in the theater and the Police Chief had to come to maintain order of the boisterous crowd. Finally, Mayor Grillasco came to the theater and promised that he would authorize use

---

[5] Ibid, 4.

[6] Ibid.

of the baseball stadium the next day. From the fourth night on, the Osborn crusade moved to the Carlos H. Terry baseball stadium and the crowds exceeded 15,000 every night. Additionally, more than 3,000 were converted with hundreds more receiving miraculous healing at every service. Among those experiencing healing were deaf-mutes, the crippled, paralytics, those with tuberculosis and those with all manner of sickness.

Eventually this baseball stadium could not hold the crowds and the meeting was moved to the Francisco (Paquito) Montaner stadium which was home to the professional baseball team the Ponce Lions. Once again, Osborn wrote:

> When the Carlos H. Terry stadium proved too small for the multitude, the larger 'Montaner' baseball stadium was secured with the intervention of the Governor of Puerto Rico [Luis Muñoz Marín]. The gates opened early and by 4:00 p.m. the stands were filled to capacity and more than 5,000 additional people were on the field of play. Roads leading to the park were jammed and hundreds of people walked to the stadium.[7]

Julia Flores

This series of meetings literally shocked the city of Ponce, and even the entire Island. People came long

---

[7] Ibid.

distances from towns across Puerto Rico to attend the meetings. Multiple healings of those who walked with

crutches were part of each service. Healings like that of Julia Flores who used her hands to push herself across the floor while dragging her legs behind her; or Juan Santos, paralyzed for 15 years, who was often seen in the streets of Ponce using a short cane and stool to get around; or María Santiago, daughter of the Chief of Police,

Juan Santos

crippled for six years, reverberated throughout the city. Osborn recalled the move of God in that city: The Police Chief stated that the sporting venues were closed, and the theaters were totally vacant; the people had abandoned the bars. The great majority of the people were at the services. The police also reported a lower number of arrests were made during the crusade services."[8]

The man who stood beside evangelist Osborn interpreting the message each night of the crusade was Reverend Antonio Collazo. This experience gave him and the Church of God *M.B.* major exposure across the entire Island. Evangelist Osborn noted the experience of preaching through an interpreter in this way:

This was the first time that I had preached with signs following the sermon where each of my prayers was interpreted into another language. Daisy and I wanted to

---

[8] Ibid., 19.

do this in India, but the traditional thinking of the missionaries there would not allow it. We believed that the funds expended to pay a language instructor could be used more effectively with a translator who could teach us the language and interpret for us during the evangelistic crusades. But our idea was rejected. We were required to focus on learning the language instead.[9]

The evangelistic ministry of T.L. Osborn was radically changed as a result of having preached with Reverend Collazo interpreting the sermon. From that point on, Brother Tony became the official Spanish interpreter for evangelist Osborn whenever he ministered in Latin America. Later on, Brother Osborn learned to speak Spanish very well. He spoke with the same inflection as Brother Tony, likely because he would make tape recordings that Osborn would listen to for hours. As a result, Osborn's Spanish accent mirrored that of Brother Tony. Later on, I had the opportunity to attend a T.L. Osborn crusade in Puerto Rico where I heard him preach in excellent Spanish.

Blind girl receives a miracle at the Osborn crusade

Following the epochal T.L. Osborn crusade, the Church of God *M.B.* saw dramatic growth under the leadership Reverend Collazo. In 1954 Reverend Miguel Navas[10]

---

[9] Ibid.

[10] Reverend Navas quickly emerged as an unquestioned leader in the Church of God *M.B.* He was a charismatic figure with a broad

joined the Church of God along with his two congregations in Caguas and Gurabo that were known as Revival Christian Church. Within a short time, through his encouragement, two additional churches located in the Jaguas de Gurabo section also joined. They were known as Christ of the Jordan church. One in the Jaguas section was pastored by Reverend Mercedes Adorno, and another in the El Peñón[11] sector pastored by Reverend Águedo Nieves. These congregations had been organized under the ministry of Juana and Segundo Torres and their son Victor Torres. Still later, another two churches from the neighborhoods of Quebrada Negrito and La Gloria (formerly Quebrada Infierno) in the town of Trujillo Alto joined.

Reverend Frank Hernández along with his congregation Iglesia Roca De Salvación, entered fellowship with the Church Of God *M.B.* in 1955 along with four churches located in Cotto Canas, Ponce; Miñe Miñe, Loiza; Vega Alta, and Guayama. By the end of that year under Brother Tony's strong leadership, the church had grown to 35 congregations with 2,561 members.

---

smile, imposing personality, and mild-mannered in his treatment of people. He was called to pastor the church at Mayor Cantera in Ponce in 1960, and in 1964 was named Educational Director of the Inter-American Bible Institute, today known as the Theological University of the Caribbean. Finally, in 1967 he was appointed Overseer of the Church of God *M.B.*, a position he held until 1978.

[11] It was at this church in 1942 that Isaías Estrada Estrada and Clotilde Adorno Flores, parents of author Wilfredo Estrada Adorno were saved.

In addition to the strong missionary and evangelistic fervor that burned in his heart, his passion for Biblical and ministerial education led him to start a school of the prophets. Brother Tony organized the Inter-American Bible Institute, now the Theological University of the Caribbean in 1956 and became its first Director. Right away he made arrangements to have Reverend William D. Alton, who was serving as missionary in the Dominican Republic, named by the Missions Department of the Church of God as the Educational Director of the Institute.

Toward the end of the 1050s two more churches united with the Church of God *M.B.* One was located in Fajardo and pastored by Reverend Antonio Flores, and the second, the Iglesia Monte de Sion in Hato Rey, was pastored by Reverend Antonio Resto Mijol. By this time the Executive Committee of the Church of God was making arrangements to have Brother Collazo assume leadership of the Hispanic work east of the Mississippi with offices in New York City.

When he left Puerto Rico in 1958 after having served as Overseer of the Island for 12 years, Brother Tony left a total of 62 churches with over 4,000 members, a strong educational program anchored in the Bible Institute, and fully functioning Departments of Youth, Ladies, and Men.[12] In other words, he left a well-organized church ready to continue its onward missionary and evangelistic march on the Island.

---

[12] "Eras de La Mies: La Iglesia de Dios Avanza Al Este Del Mississippi," *El Evangelio*, March 1965, 8.

In chapter six we will examine Reverend Collazo's responsibilities as Overseer of the Eastern Spanish District of the Church of God based in New York City. Onward!

Chapter 6

Return to New York as Overseer of the Eastern Spanish District of the Church of God

In the Fall of 1954 Following the Church of God General Assembly, Reverend Henry C. Stoppe who had served as Superintendent of the West Indies (the work in the Caribbean), was transferred to be Overseer of New York and New Jersey. He was also assigned oversight of the Spanish work east of the Mississippi. Since he did not speak Spanish he named Reverend Samuel Irizarry as Secretary for the Spanish work. In reality, he functioned as overseer of the Spanish churches during the period that they reported to Reverend Stoppe.

The first evangelistic outreach of the Church of God into the Spanish community developed in New York City. It is interesting to note that the person who was at the forefront of this effort to organize the church there was not a minister of the Church of God. I refer to the Reverend Juan L. Lugo.

The second push to reach Puerto Ricans in the United States was the city of Chicago. The leaders of the missionary and evangelistic outreach there were Felipe Montañez and Tomás de Jesús, among others. The Puerto Rican community in Chicago came predominately from the city of Manatí and the surrounding area, evangelized by pastor Ángel Berganzo, a recognized leader of the Church of God *M.B.* in the north of the Island, and his church in Coto Norte.

The Collazo-Lugo family with Rev. Juan L. Lugo and Sis. Isabelita Ortiz-Lugo

Dr. Esdras Betancourt recounts that near the time of the 1958 General Assembly the small group of pastors of the Spanish churches in the eastern district requested "a bilingual or Hispanic overseer to lead the work."[1] This was the circumstance that led to the appointment of Reverend Antonio Collazo as Overseer of the Eastern Spanish District of the Church of God at that General Assembly. After twelve wonderfully fruitful years of pastoral and supervisory ministry in Puerto Rico, the Church of God Executive Committee

---

[1] Ibid., 71.

called him to assume leadership of the Spanish churches east of the Mississippi River. Once again the Collazo family prepared to move to the city of skyscrapers. The picture shown here was taken as the family prepared to leave for New York City in 1958.

The groundwork for what was to become the Eastern Spanish District of the Church of God was laid in 1948 as a result of the initiative of the pioneer Pentecostal missionary to Puerto Rico, Juan L. Lugo. Interestingly, this leader who was involved with the start of the Pentecostal Church of God, Inc. under the auspices of the Assemblies of God on the Island and also supervised the Assemblies churches in New York for a year, was additionally part of the start of the work of the Church of God among Spanish churches east of the Mississippi River. The historian of the Hispanic Church of God in the United States Dr. Betancourt says:

> The Spanish First Pentecostal Church, known today as the Church of God of Third Avenue (Manhattan), which was pastored at that time by Pentecostal pioneer Juan L. Lugo and his wife Isabel played a crucial role in the initial development of our organization. While the church did not formally belong to the denomination, it was a very important part of the growth of the ministry in the region by sponsoring ministers who came from Puerto Rico to New York to start new works.[2]

Among the ministers who received a warm helping hand from Brother Lugo were the following pastors: Ángel

---

[2] Betancourt, *En el espíritu y poder de pentecostés*, 69.

and Emma Betancourt,[3] Saturnino and Francisca Rodríguez, and Victor Duran. Brother Betancourt began his work as a church planter on 105th Street in Spanish Harlem in 1948. Historian Betancourt talking about his father's ministry indicated that Brother Ángel (as he was affectionately known) "when his friend Saturnino Rodríguez arrived from Puerto Rico seeking a better life, he turned over the church on 105th Street to him and went on planting churches in Lower Manhattan where he lived."[4]

When Brother Collazo arrived in New York to assume his new duties as Overseer there were some 7 churches in the area. Once again, he started working in the region east of the Mississippi just as he had in Puerto Rico in 1946. Now, 12 years after he started with a small group on the Island that had grown exponentially under his leadership, he begins again – with his wife Pérsida and family – to work as a Church of God missionary, this time in the eastern United States. Brother Tony did not complain or back down from the new challenge facing him and began his new task with the same confidence in his God as he did in Puerto Rico. There were many years of sowing and hoping, but in its time this missionary and evangelistic effort produced its fruit.

The churches that Brother Tony found in the area designated as the Eastern Spanish District which included the states of New York, New Jersey, Connecticut,

---

[3] This couple were the parents of Dr. Esdras Betancourt, pastor and educational leader of the Church of God in the USA for nearly six decades

[4] Betancourt, *En el espíritu y poder de pentecostés*, 70.

-1970 Members of the Mission Board 1968

Massachusetts, Maine, Vermont, New Hampshire, Rhode Island, Pennsylvania, Ohio, Indiana, Illinois, Michigan, Maryland, Washington D.C., Georgia, and Florida were all located in New York. These were: 100th Street (originally 105th Street started in 1948 by Rev. Ángel Betancourt), 6th Street organized by Ángel M. Díaz, Third Avenue pastored by Rev. Juan Lugo, Brook Avenue pastored by Rev. Saturnino Rodríguez, Crotona Avenue pastored by Dámaso Acevedo, Johnson Avenue pastored by Victor Durán, and Sackman Avenue.[5]

Seven years after his tenure began as Overseer of the Eastern Spanish District, Brother Collazo led 40 congregations, most of which worshipped in their own facilities where they fulfilled their evangelistic mission. In New York alone, 23 congregations had been started. In 1966 he was named to the Mission Board of the Church of God. He was the first Hispanic to ever occupy that position.

At the General Assembly In 1970, Brother Collazo ended his tenure as Overseer of the Eastern Spanish District. He was appointed as Overseer of the Spanish churches in the South Central Region based in San Antonio, Texas. Upon his departure from the work in the

---

[5] I have relied on the extraordinary contribution of Dr. Esdras Betancourt in reconstructing this historical data. Ibid., 69-77.

eastern half of the country, the Spanish publication *El Evangelio* included the following describing his ministry: "His work in the states east of the Mississippi was so fruitful that, when he departed, the churches were financially self-supporting and no longer needed to rely on the General Offices for support."[6]

In chapter seven we will accompany Brother and Sister Collazo to their new assignment as Overseer of the South Central Region. This would be his final assignment as an Overseer in the Church of God before his retirement. We will follow this spiritual giant and this heroine of the faith in the work where he was called to pastor and supervise another group of ministers in both a new geographical and cultural context. So then, let us move on to San Antonio, Texas and the South Central Region!

---

[6] "El Rdo. Antonio Collazo Ha Vencido La Muerte," *El Evangelio*, n.d., 34–35.

Chapter 7

Ministry in the South Central Region of the Church of God Based in San Antonio, Texas

The Church of God Mission Board named Reverend Collazo as Overseer of the South Central Region in 1970. It had been established in 1968 with the dividing of the Region West of the Mississippi into two separate areas. The Western Region was led by Reverend Josué B. Rubio and the South Central Region by Reverend Noel de Souza, who served for two years. The states encompassed by this region were: Texas, New Mexico, Oklahoma, Colorado, Kansas, Arkansas, and Louisiana, with a total of 12 churches. There were six in San Antonio, two in Houston, with one each in New Mexico, West Dallas, Denver, and New Orleans. It was with this small nucleus of churches that Brother Tony began his tenure in the South Central region.

After receiving his new assignment at the 1970 General Assembly, Brother Tony briefly returned to New York to bid farewell to the ministers and churches of the Eastern Spanish District. He left behind a 12 year legacy of fruitful labor. When he arrived in 1958 there were seven churches. Now upon his departure, the territory was self-sufficient with nearly 50 churches. His untiring work and warm treatment of the ministers had resulted in a plentiful harvest.

When Brother Tony arrived in San Antonio to assume leadership of the South Central Region he saw a challenging task ahead in this new area. The division of the larger Spanish ministry west of the Mississippi resulted in the South Central Region having fewer churches – a total of 12 – than the Western Region. He immediately began to devise a strategy of expand the outreach into the larger cities of the Territory.

One of his first endeavors was the further development of the Church of God in Dallas. It came about when three families from Denver, Colorado and San Antonio moved there. These were families with great missionary zeal who set out to plant a church in this great city, and that is how the work in Dallas began. Sister Ninfa Beltrán Ramírez[1] provided me a written document that described the beginning of the Dallas church.

Brother Ignacio Beltrán and his wife Trinidad attended the Foursquare Church in Denver, Colorado before moving to Dallas, Texas in 1964. He loved to preach the Word, and she was well known for her desire to win souls to the Lord through her testimony from the time of her conversion in 1957 in Denver.

---

[1] Sister Ninfa Beltrán Ramírez is the daughter of Ignacio and Trinidad Beltrán. She serves alongside her husband, Reverend Carlos Ramírez as pastors of a church in Dallas.

As a result of her witnessing, she met Sister Angélica García and Sister Losoya who had moved to Dallas from San Antonio. When Sister Beltrán asked them if they knew the Lord Jesus, they quickly replied "yes" although it did not appear that they attended any church at the time. They explained that they attended the Church of God in San Antonio but were disappointed that they could not find one in Dallas. And so, together, Sister García, Sister Losoya, and the Beltrán family began to hold services in the home of Sister García. These were the first three families that met together to worship the Lord and start the Church of God in Dallas toward the end of 1965. While they continued witnessing they also told the people of a new Spanish church in the community. The numbers increased to the point that it became necessary to move the congregation to a larger place. They rented a duplex on Florence Street in central Dallas and knocked out the walls to make room for a small sanctuary. They also bought an old piano, pulpit, and chairs.

At that time the Overseer of the Territory was Brother Josué Beltrán Rubio, and he was contacted to let him know about the growing mission and of the need for a pastor. Since Brother Ignacio Beltrán served on an interim basis, Pastor Moisés Aparicio was sent from San Antonio in October of 1967 to assume the pastorate in Dallas.

The church continued to grow and about six months later, had the opportunity to purchase a church building at 4402 Roseland. Three years later, Pastor Aparicio resigned and started a second church on Herbert Street which today is the Word of Life Church of God. Reverend David Hernández assumed pastorate of the church on Roseland followed by interim pastor Robert Palomo, and later by Reverend Adolfo De La Garza, Sr. in August 1972.

The third Church of God – Love Field – was planted by Brother and Sister Beltrán in 1973. They also planted another three churches in the Dallas area. The fourth church, the Church of God at Munger Place was planted by Pastor Robert Palomo.[2]

Other champions were added to the work in Dallas by Brother Tony along with these first Church of God pioneers, among them was Adolfo de la Garza, Sr. from Laredo in 1972. He was part of a ministerial family committed to the ministry of the Church of God. In describing his ministry to me, Dr. Fidencio Burgueño, Administrative Bishop of the South Central Region said the following:

> According to his sons, Pastor de la Garza developed an outreach strategy that encompassed the four major areas of the city; north Dallas, South Dallas, east Dallas, and west Dallas. Later it included Mesquite and Garland. Now some fifty years later we have churches in all of those areas and nearly 60 churches in Metro Dallas-Fort Worth. Obviously, the de la Garza family has been instrumental in the development of the work of the Church of God in Dallas. However, it was the parents of

---

[2] This was the response from Sister Ninfa Beltrán Ramírez to the author's question about the beginning of the Church of God work in Dallas. June 29, 2017.

Sister Ninfa Beltrán Ramírez who were the real pioneers and founded many of the churches in the Dallas area. They were not pastors and did not have ministerial credentials, but Sister Ninfa's mother have a deep fervor and charismatic personality. Her evangelistic work attracted new people to the church who accepted the Lord, and in turn invited others to come. In that way the gospel was spread throughout the city of Dallas.[3]

It was to this South Central Region, with churches primarily in San Antonio and Dallas that the seasoned and experienced Antonio Collazo came to serve as Overseer in 1970. Regarding his influence in this newly created territory, Reverend Antonino Bonilla, who succeeded Brother Tony as Administrative Bishop there in 1976, told me the following:

Brother Collazo's influence was crucial in establishing new congregations. His vast experience gained from work as a pastor, teacher, and administrator served him well in advancing the evangelistic outreach in the Region. His warm and appealing personality helped him exercise a strong and effective leadership in his supervisory work with the wholehearted support of the pastors and leaders who constituted the ministry of the South Central Region.[4]

---

[3] In order to reconstruct this period, I relied on the help of Dr. Fidencio Burgueño, Administrative Bishop of the South Central Region in an interview on June 4, 2017.

[4] Bonilla interview.

Ministry in the South Central Region

The administrative skills that Brother Tony brought to his work, along with his winsome approach toward the pastors was a crucial factor in the growth of the Region. Today it is one of the strongest areas of Church of God Hispanic ministry in the United States both in terms of number of churches and finances.

Part of his supervisory strategy was to keep the ministers informed of events in the Region. He did this by creating a newsletter called *El Noticiero* (The News) where he reported the growth of the area, his administrative activity, and the various achievements of the churches. In one of the last editions, when he knew he would retire from his position as Overseer of the South Central Region, he wrote to his pastors:

> As most of you already know, I your servant will be entering retirement at the end of the upcoming General Assembly. On the last day of that meeting I hope to meet with you all to introduce you to your newly appointed Overseer. I will be delighted to see all or as many of the ministers of the Region who can attend on that day.[5]

In his typically gentle and sensitive way Brother Tony began preparing his fellow laborers in ministry for the leadership change that would soon come to the Central Territory, which would later be designated the South Central Region. Following the General Assembly in 1976, Brother Tony passed the torch of leadership to his

---

[5] Antonio Collazo, "Estadísticas de Junio, Iglesia de Dios Territorio Sur Central Hispano," *El Noticiero*, June 1976, 1.

successor Reverend Antonino Bonilla. The June 1976 edition of *El Noticiero* reported that there were 18 churches in the Region. Finally, at age 66 and after 38 years of fruitful ministry as pastor, teacher, interpreter, administrator, and mentor, Reverend Antonio Collazo retired as a minister in the Church of God, but he did not retire from ministry. As a matter of fact, when an unexpected vacancy occurred in the North Central Region in 1983, Overseer Cecil B. Knight asked Brother Collazo to fill in as Interim Overseer for that Region, which he did for the period of a year.

Next we will revisit the educational and pastoral ministry of Brother Tony. We will do this by inviting him to speak directly to us through a series of his articles and sermons. Get ready for an amazing journey from the pen of this special teacher/preacher. I encourage you to slowly unravel the thread of the next chapter and savor the inspired teaching contained therein. Onward!

Chapter 8

The Teacher and Preacher

In this chapter I will highlight Reverend Antonio Collazo's role as preacher and teacher. Brother Tony was a unique Pentecostal preacher. His manner of preaching was not that of the typical Pentecostal preacher who was often loud and boisterous. However, he was powerfully persuasive in his preaching with exquisite content in his sermons. His deep spirituality was evident by the anointing and authority from on high in his preaching.

In the same way, he was a teacher par excellence. His preparation for teaching was superb and he captivated his audience. I will highlight some of his teaching and sermon materials in this chapter to provide a sense of the superior quality of his work. Doctor Fidencio Burgueño shared these thoughts about Brother Tony's preaching and teaching: "I remember him as an excellent preacher whose sermons were very focused and clear. He was also an extraordinary teacher whose material was always well outlined.

Brother Tony did not yell a lot, but he said a lot. That had a great impact on me both in his preaching and teaching."[1]

With this brief introduction I want to move on to Reverend Antonio Collazo's sermons and teaching. This is a sampling of his work, and I especially thank Dr. Carlos Moran, Director of Editorial Evangélica for his willingness to allow me to share some of Brother Tony's articles that appeared in several editions of *El Evangelio*, the monthly publication for the Spanish speaking constituency of the Church of God. The sermons that I include in this chapter are provided by Pérsida (Tita) Collazo Pagan, daughter of Tony and Pérsida Collazo. My sincere appreciation goes out to both Carlos and Tita for their support.

Let us now enjoy the wisdom of this true apostle. We begin with six articles written by Brother Tony and published over a period of years.

Pentecost with Purpose[2]

By Antonio Collazo

IN THE COMMENTARY ON THE ASSIGNED TOPIC: "Pentecost with Purpose," we will explore the functions of prophet and pastor in fulfilling the purpose of Pentecost. We believe that the best way to consider this important subject is to review the work of the Holy Spirit from the beginning.

---

[1] Burgueño interview.

[2] Antonio Collazo, "Pentecostés Con Propósito," *El Evangelio*, June 1976, 9–11.

We can affirm about God the Father and God the Holy Spirit the same thing that Hebrews 13:8 declares about God the Son. "Jesus Christ is the same yesterday and today and forever." Therefore, we believe that one makes a critical error if we refer to the work of the Holy Spirit as if He was born on the Day of Pentecost. It would be like considering the redemptive work of Christ as if His existence began at His virgin birth in Bethlehem of Judea.

We can summarize the above by stating that God the Father, God the Son, and God the Holy Spirit are one from eternity to eternity. Speaking of the Son, John wrote in his Gospel: "In the beginning was the Word, and the Word was with God, and the Word was God" (John 1:1 NIV).

When John says that the Word was with God, he is including God the Father and God the Holy Spirit. That being said, we can only conclude that there is no way to perceive of a triune God where each of the Persons in that Godhead would act independently from the others in their own authority or will. Neither can we see in this Triune God each Person acting under specific and definitive orders from another member of the Trinity.

When we say, "I believe in one God eternally existing in three Divine Persons, namely, Father, Son, and Holy Spirit," we are thinking of one omnipotent God with each member of the Trinity acting in complete harmony and agreement with the other two. This is the same as saying that what the Father does aligns with the will of the Son and the Holy Spirit; what the Son does aligns with the will of the Father and the Holy Spirit; and what the Holy Spirit does aligns with the will of the Father and the Son.

There is no better example than the scene at the Jordan River, on the day Jesus was baptized by John the Baptist, to illustrate this truth. "As soon as Jesus was baptized, he went up out of the water. At that moment heaven was opened, and he saw the Spirit of God descending like a dove and alighting on him. And a voice from heaven said, 'This is my Son, whom I love; with him I am well pleased.'" (Matthew 3:16,17 NIV).

Throughout the Old Testament we find the Holy Spirit working and manifesting Himself in different periods. There was always a reason for this and the objective of the manifestation was always achieved (Genesis 1:2; 1 Samuel 10:6, 10; Judges 3:10, 34; 11:29; 13:25;14:6, 20; 1 Samuel 11:6; 16:13; Ezekiel 37:11, 43:5).

The preceding discussion should lead us to avoid the error of considering the Holy Spirit in His work as a mere influence or agent operating under specific orders. Rather it should logically lead us to the firm conclusion that the Holy Spirit is the same in substance, and equal in power and glory to the Father and the Son. Based on this truth, we shall now address the theme of this article, Pentecost with Purpose.

We begin by restating the subject as follows: God the Holy Spirit was manifested at Pentecost for a specific purpose. The New Testament contains manifestations of the Holy Spirit before the Day of Pentecost. He performed an important function at the incarnation of the Word (Luke 1:35). He anointed Jesus' human nature so that He could resist temptation in order to remain pure and without blemish. This made it possible that the pure and unblemished blood shed from a pure and unblemished body could blot out the sins of the contaminated and dirty soul of the sinner, sowing instead the seed for the birth of a pure and spotless body at the resurrection.

Pentecost denoted the beginning of a new manifestation or ministry that was different from the sporadic or occasional appearances of the Holy Spirit prior to that day. At Pentecost the Holy Spirit, from that time forward, was fully and permanently present in the world with and in the church. He edifies, empowers and will totally prepare the church for the day when He presents it to Christ as a suitable bride without spot or blemish (Ephesians 5:27).

While achieving this primary objective, additional and equally important tasks emerge. Just as God fulfills His purpose to save us through the manifestation of God the Son by the seed of a woman, so too God fulfills His purpose to perfect and prepare the church through the manifestation of God the Holy Spirit in and through the seed of Christ, who we are as believers.

Some of the additional functions of the Holy Spirit in the believer include regeneration, sanctification, helps, enduement with power or baptism, choosing and calling, much like the allocation of ministry to those who are called. Also, are the equipping and preparation for effective operation of ministry, for imparting of insight (John 14:26), and for the operation of the gifts of the Spirit (1 Corinthians 12:6-10).

Of the various ministry functions mentioned in Ephesians 4:11-12, two we referred to earlier, prophets and pastors, come to mind. First let us consider the ministry of the prophet. A prophet may be described as one who is divinely inspired to communicate the will of God to His people, and to declare the future. The Hebrew word for prophet is "nabi" which is derived from the verb "naba" which is translated "to announce." Thus, one refers to a prophet as a person who is called to declare, or one who announces.

Much like the prophets or preachers, we are men and women called and commissioned by the Holy Spirit to announce or communicate the message of God. God has recorded everything that He wants us to know about the past, present, and future in His holy Word.

Today, all that you must do in order to be a prophet is to preach the Word of God. Whether as a pastor, evangelist, doctor, deacon, or lay person, if you preach the Word you are a prophet. We have said, **if you preach the Word.** The most eloquently presented sermon, if it lacks the Word and the anointing of the Holy Spirit, is simply dry, vain, and ineffective. Conversely, the sermon presented using the simplest language with possibly incorrect grammar, if grounded and infused with the Word, and under the anointing of the Holy Spirit, will be edifying, convincing, and effective.

As a prophet, give attention to preach the Word with the same awareness and aim that Paul advised Timothy when he wrote: "Do your best to present yourself to God as one approved, a worker who does not need to be ashamed and who correctly handles the word of truth" (2 Timothy 2:15 NIV). When you preach, do so aware that you are fulfilling the ministry of prophet to which God the Holy Spirit has called and commissioned you. Be a good prophet; be a good preacher.

Now let us consider the ministry of a pastor. Pastor: "One who serves and watches over." We can better understand this definition by observing the routine of a shepherd. In the morning he takes the sheep out of the sheepfold. He does this by getting in front of them and calling them in a manner that they already understand. He leads them to the pasture and there, while they eat, he watches over and makes sure that none of them strays too far from the flock or is attacked by wild animals.

Should one go astray because of his inattention or any other reason, the shepherd diligently searches until he finds it and returns it to the fold. Then at the appropriate time he leads them to water. Later in the day he returns them to the sheepfold, carefully noting that all are inside before shutting the door. Finally, he stands guard during the night so that no wolf or lion will jump the fence to attack the sheep. This shows that the shepherd serves 24 hours a day. Consider how the *Living Bible* renders Ephesians 4:11. "...others have a gift for caring for God's people as a shepherd does his sheep, leading and teaching them in the ways of God."

Let us reflect upon the reality that the call to be a pastor and the pastoral ministry is the most important work with which God the Holy Spirit entrusts us. The Bible says: "Be shepherds of God's flock that is under your care, watching over them—not because you must, but because you are willing, as God wants you to be; not pursuing dishonest gain, but eager to serve; not lording it over those entrusted to you, but being examples to the flock" (1 Peter 5:2, 3).

This passage alone does not capture the complexity of this ministry that the Holy Spirit has charged us to fulfill. As challenging as the pastoral ministry is, the majority of the other ministries described in the New Testament are connected to it. So, the pastor is faced with the daunting task of incorporating these disparate roles into a unified ministry. Sometimes he asks himself, do I have one ministry or many? Am I a pastor or an administrator? Am I a teacher, evangelist, or devotional leader?

Enmeshed in this complex problem that the pastor faces is the following dilemma. Does the idealized expectation of the parishioners align with the reality of whether the pastor is adequately prepared for the task at hand? The pastor is expected to produce challenging sermons in each service and to teach with eloquence and brilliance. Sometimes he must serve as a contractor, laborer, plumber, custodian, and even on some occasions as a taxi service. Consequently, the pastor can become confused trying to fulfill the expected role while being diverted into other roles that serve to detract from the primary pastoral function.

As a result of this frustrating commitment – of conforming to the expected role – the pastor often finds himself over emphasizing the area in which he feels most comfortable and competent while overlooking other important responsibilities of his task. The outcome often is a falling apart of the Christian witness because of a failure to maintain balance in the pastoral function.

From a theological perspective, the role of the pastor is mapped out in the rural and nomadic life of the Shepherd illustrated in Psalm 23. Jeremiah sees the pastors assigned by God to watch over His people (Jeremiah 23:2). In the New Testament, Christ is the Good Shepherd, caring for the wounded like the Good Samaritan did, and searching for the lost sheep leaving the ninety and nine in the sheep-fold.

Stir Up the Gift of God[3]

By Antonio Collazo

"I am reminded of your sincere faith, which first lived in your grandmother Lois

And in your mother Eunice and, I am persuaded, now lives in you also.

For this reason, I remind you to fan into flame the gift of God,

Which is in you through the laying on of my hands" (2 Timothy 1:5, 6 NIV).

THESE WORDS WERE WRITTEN by the elderly Apostle Paul while he listened to the file that sharpened the axe that would be used to execute him. Sitting there, he faced the end of his earthly journey knowing that his voice would soon be silenced. He stood between two worlds. On the one hand, he felt a great longing to continue the work he had started. On the other, he desired to rest from the exhausting effort. He was keenly aware that he would soon face the executioner who would cut off his head. It

---

[3] Antonio Collazo, "Despierta El Don de Dios," *El Evangelio*, October 1976, 16.

was because of his Christian witness that he would die, but that witness would reach far beyond the walls of the prison.

He wrote to Timothy: "For I am now ready to be offered, and the time of my departure is at hand. I have fought a good fight, I have finished *my* course, I have kept the faith:" (2 Timothy 4:6, 7 KJV). This writing from death row had the ring of finality. It was almost as if he was speaking of his life in the past tense.

But Paul did not stop there. He added the word "Henceforth" which means "from this point on." In his words, "I am passing from a world of limitations to a world grace." However, he never lost his passion for the church and his mission on the earth. While he waited at the threshold of the other world, he provided instructions for the well-being of those for whom he was responsible.

His only hope of seeing the work move forward in its original power and glory was to fan the flame in the life of those he had taught. In the past, he was committed to light the fire; he had provided the fuel with which to keep it burning perpetually. Now, at the point of his own death, he needs to act in a positive and appealing way to rekindle the embers in the lives of those who were complacent.

Determined as he was in the face of coming obstacles and opposition that awaited the doctrine, he could not condemn the complacency of any man. However, with head held high, he confidently said: "I was not disobedient to the vision from heaven" (Acts 26:19 NIV). Having such a strong example to follow, it was very difficult for his fellow laborers to be less fervent. He could not reconcile the reality of a perishing world with the idea of weak workers.

Paul challenges Timothy, "Do not neglect the gift that is in you, which was given to you by prophecy with the laying on of the hands of the eldership" (1 Timothy 4:14 NIV). It is important to firmly believe and be persuaded by the doctrine. This is fundamental to the development of the believer. However, this is not enough in order to complete the task at hand. Accepting the truth of the doctrine should be the first step. Simply remaining quiet in the personal assurance of grace is to minimize the required militant effort.

There should be a stirring in the heart of a Christian to put into action the talent, gifts, sense of compassion, and determination to hold the line against those forces that array themselves in opposition to the church. The old Apostle felt the pressure of each moment that passed. Every minute presented greater threats against the Christian cause. Apostasy was gaining ground.

Paul writes this letter to Timothy with a sense of urgency. That is why he says: "For this reason I remind you to fan into flame the gift of God, which is in you through the laying on of my hands" (2 Timothy 1:6 NIV). In this he reminds the young minister of the day of his ordination. He hopes to renew the momentum and the ministerial flame that Timothy demonstrated in the early days of his ministry. Possibly, he recalled the questions he answered for his ordination like: "Do you believe that Jesus is the Son of God?, Do you accept without reservation the doctrine of the Apostles according to the faith given through

Christ?, Will you defend it against all heresy?, Will you keep this teaching as your daily guide?, and above all else, Are you filled with the Holy Spirit?

Paul was a fearless warrior in his day. Nobody challenged his position. The Pentecostal Power was the moving force in his life, but the time of his departure, as he himself says in his letter to Timothy, was at hand.

Bringing this story forward into our time, we can see Paul as representative of the founders of the church today. Timothy represents those to whom the torch of Truth has been passed, not only the clergy, but all who take responsibility for the church in these the last days. Much like Paul we can say that the time of our departure is near. The necessity to energize all of our spiritual energy is no less than now that it was then. The dangers of apostasy are even more prevalent today than in the days of Paul.

The dangers are greater because of the brevity of the time left. We do not see the extreme mass crime of believers being martyred now as in times past. However, the threat in our day is the creeping revolution that seeks to erode the spirituality of the church. It is like a war of germs that sap the strength and neutralize the implements used to fight them. An attitude of appeasement prevails until the white flag of surrender is finally raised.

It is time to rise up and consider the circumstances that surround us. Examine yourself, take stock of your own provision and judge your spiritual condition. Honor God and ask yourself the question: "Do I have the same enthusiasm and spiritual commitment as in earlier days?" if you can answer in the affirmative, rejoice, if not, then you have reason to pray fervently until it returns.

We might measure our spiritual condition by answering questions such as, Does the Word of God move me as in the past? Am I determined to live a life of holiness like before? Do I attend church with the same devotion as in the beginning? Do I still feel the same passion for souls and continue to evangelize? Does the Spirit of God move me as in the past?

If we consider our current situation in light of the above questions and discover that we fall short in some area, then it is time to gather the coals covered with ash and to once again fan the flame of a victorious life. We are in the final days of the Dispensation of Grace so that what remains to do must be done quickly.

These are the days that Paul describes to Timothy when he says, "They will turn their ears away from the truth and turn aside to myths" (2 Timothy 4:4 NIV). The implication is that they once walked in the Truth. Sadly, we see these things happening today; the attitude described by the Apostle John in revelation is very much in evidence in our day.

Clearly if the men and women of our day are to be persuaded to accept Christ, there needs to be a change in our passive attitude. We need an active resurgence in our commitment to pray and intercede, to faithful service by those whom God has called to minister, as well as openness to the moving of the old power of Pentecost in our lives.

The prophet Joel describes the dramatic change from complacency to combat when he says, "Proclaim this among the nations: Prepare for war! Rouse the warriors! Let all the fighting men draw near and attack. Beat your plowshares into swords and your pruning hooks into spears. Let the weakling say, 'I am strong!'" (Joel 3:9-10 NIV).

There are multitudes "in the valley of decision" who could well be won to Christ with renewed effort. That is why it is necessary for each of us to heed the advice of the Apostle: "Fan into flame the gift of God which is in you..." and to do our part in the great task of evangelizing the world.

Evangelism in the Home[4]

By Antonio Collazo

"For I have chosen him, so that he will direct his children and his household after him to keep the way of the LORD by doing what is right and just, so that the LORD will bring about for Abraham what he has promised him" (Genesis 18:19 NIV).

AT THE DAWN OF CREATION God instituted the home. Therefore, it is a holy institution and should be a place of peace and happiness, even though that is often not the case. Homes break up daily and many of those that remain do not make even the slightest effort to please God. Why

---

[4] Antonio Collazo, "Evangelismo En El Hogar," *El Evangelio*, November 1976, 4–5.

is this so? The answer is quite simple: there is very little time or space in most homes given to **evangelism**.

Many homes are characterized by distractions such as drinking, fighting, partying, and sports to the point where there is no time left to address the importance of living according to the Word of God. Even in church-going families time is not taken for reading and studying the Bible. In some instances, time is not taken to even thank God for the food and provision that He provides. We are so busy pushing our children to succeed in the world, that we cannot find time to evangelize our own home.

Many children choose the ways of the world because there is no Christian model in the home. Often both the Word and a good example are lacking. If we really want to evangelize our homes, each of our actions, words, looks, and conversations should be carefully measured. Many parents have the courage to criticize the Supreme Court for banning Bible reading and prayer in the public schools and that is certainly something worth protesting. However, it is also true that these same parents do not have the courage to wipe the dust from the family Bible so that it can come alive in the hearts of their children.

In the text mentioned earlier, we hear God say: "For I have chosen him, so that he will direct his children and his household after him" (another translation says: "For I know him..." KJV). What does God know about you as a parent? God had confidence that Abraham would evangelize his home, not with a heavy hand or with fury, but in the power of a life that was characterized by righteousness, holiness and consistency.

Many children have never heard their father or mother pray in the home. The expectation being that this training was what only the church should do, when in fact this should be the principal responsibility of the home.

Life begins in the home. It is the most influential institution in the world. The first three to five years in the life of a child set the pattern for their behavior. That being the case, would you agree that evangelism in the home is of great value? There is an old proverb that says: "Saving the homes, saves the nation." What can we say about our own homes? Let us determine now, before it is too late, that winning our children to Christ is the greatest need in the world today.

Evangelism in the home is an obligation

God says: "These commandments that I give you today are to be on your hearts. Impress them on your children. Talk about them when you sit at home and when you walk along the road, when you lie down and when you get up" (Deuteronomy 6:6-7 NIV). Whether we want to accept it or not, we are responsible for our children. There are some things we can entrust to our neighbors, the school, or the church, but it is we ourselves who are responsible to evangelize our children. One of the reasons that the jails and orphanages are full while the Sunday Schools are empty is because we have failed to fulfill our responsibility.

Many parents have so completely compromised with sin that their children cannot tell which is the true path to follow. These parents, possibly without realizing it, are pushing their children toward a world of sin. Often they complain about how the church is losing its young people. If we really want our children to be saved, we must begin in the home. Joshua understood that evangelism in the home was his responsibility when he said: "But as for me and my household, we will serve the LORD" (Joshua 24:15 NIV).

Evangelism in the Home offers a Future for our Youth

How far can the youth of our generation really broaden their lives when their homes are not evangelized? Many homes are like crazy houses: crazy for pleasure, crazy about sports, crazy about acquiring money. Prayer is rarely (or perhaps never) heard there. God is considered as outdated or irrelevant. In many supposedly Biblical homes parents are often spiritually cold, careless and indifferent. What we need is more homes where there is a true hunger and thirst for a move of God.

The youth of our day are faced with a world in crisis; a world at the crossroads: either it gets better, or it completely destroys itself. They are faced with a world that is morally corrupt, socially sick, politically confused, and spiritually anemic. In many homes sin has become an imaginary thing, hell a joke, and the church a hobby.

We have weakened our moral principles and are quickly becoming like other nations that have failed. We sow our seed to the wind and are reaping the whirlwind. If we are to save our children and offer them a brighter future, then we need an old-time revival in our homes.

Evangelism in the Home Results in Revival in the Church

As the life in the home goes, so will the life of the church. Modernism in the home will bring modernism to the church. While our homes beget lust, and vices, and crime, and hatred and mistrust; while the divorce mills continue to erode the very foundation of our nation, our homes are in desperate need of evangelism.

If we want our churches to be aflame with the fire of God, that fire must begin in the homes of the people of God. Every father is obligated to win his family to Christ and His church. We cannot depend on others for this. We must do it ourselves. When the Christian home awakens, faith is revived, and we begin to do the things of first importance. Then the church will no longer be a "valley of dry bones" as in Ezekiel's vision. It will become a source of power, a soul saving station, and a place of worship and fellowship for the community.

Must the Lord wait in vain for the home to fill the void? The hour is late; hell is aflame. The devil is busily working toward his goal of destroying our loved ones. What are you doing to evangelize your home?

Revival among the Gentiles started in a home; the home of Cornelius (Acts 10). From there it reached the entire Gentile world. So, let us, Christian fathers and mothers commit to the evangelization of our own homes. The awakening that follows will spread to the church, the community, and to the entire nation. We will defeat Satan and win our children to the Lord and his church.

The Verbal Inspiration of the Bible[5]

By Antonio Collazo

The Sacred Scriptures are recognized as the true fountain of Christian theology. They chronicle the story of Christianity and are the repository of Divine revelation. Therefore, it is necessary to investigate the authority of Holy Scripture and to evaluate its authenticity as the true record of the historical development and completed product of Divine revelation. The matter to consider is how the Scriptures came to constitute the very Word of God.

We believe that this authority rests upon the fact that Holy Scripture is an inspired revelation for mankind. What we mean by revelation is that it was a direct communication between God and humanity of such magnitude, that it was well beyond human ability to secure. Inspiration then, is the enabling power of the Holy Spirit through which holy men were able to receive the true word and to communicate it free of error. Dr. Orlon Wiley said: "The declaration of the mind of God to man is *revelation* when it is considered from the perspective of discovered truth. It is *inspiration,* from a theological perspective, when it proceeded from the Holy Spirit and enabled those men who wrote the Bible in such a flawless way that what they wrote came to be the very declaration of God's will for humanity."

The Church of God believes that all of the Bible is completely inspired. We believe that the Bible is the written

---

[5] Antonio Collazo, "La Inspiración Verbal de La Biblia," *El Evangelio*, February 1982.

Word of God and the very Word of God. We understand that *inspiration signifies that God breathed, or what is the same, the breath of God.* The supernatural breath of God rested on the physical senses of holy men. That inspiration of God was so absolute, that what was written is indeed the supreme truth of God. Our position is that under such perfect inspiration of the Holy Spirit, and using their individual style and vocabulary, the Biblical writers gave us the Word of God. Therefore, we hold that the very words employed in the record of Scripture are inspired. This is *verbal or plenary inspiration.*

We believe that the entire Bible is inspired by God. The agnostic objects to the divine origin of Scripture and accepts it only as lofty literature. The religious liberal will only affirm that the Bible merely contains the word of God. Evangelical Christians, however, believe that the whole Bible is inspired. We believe that all of the Scriptures, as originally written, are living oracles from God and should be accepted as such.

We reject the notion that the writers of Scripture relied on spiritual sensitivity or aesthetics. Neither do we accept the theory that God revealed His truth to holy men and left it up to them to use whatever expression they chose. However, we cannot subscribe to the idea that these writers were merely robots to whom God dictated each word. "Holy men of God spoke as they were moved by the Holy Spirit" (2 Peter 1:21 NKJV). The variety of styles throughout Scripture emphasizes the fact of individual expression. We believe that this expression is inspired. What was written by men was written from God.

As such, the Bible id God's revelation of Himself to men. The story begins in Genesis chapter 1 with the account of God as creator of all things. It ends in Revelation 22 with the manifestation of Christ as the Son of God who will come soon to rule the entire universe. Between beginning and end is the beautifully fascinating story of God and His love for His people.

For some 2500 years after creation, there was no written law. Apparently, God was pleased to express His will verbally and directly through individuals such as Adam (Genesis 2:16); Noah (Genesis 6:13); Abraham (Genesis 12:1) and many others. So, it appears that from the beginning God instructed man with regard to many precepts that were later incorporated into the Law. Some of these included the Sabbath (Genesis 2:2); sacrifices (Genesis 4:4) and the respect for life and property (Genesis4:10, 11).

In addition to the Bible, mankind also relies on two independent witnesses. First, the work of creation or the natural world (Psalm 19:1) and second, our conscience (Romans 2:14, 15). Before there was a written law, humans apparently maintained a relationship with God by the dictates of conscience, but man eventually failed in his conscience. That precious and priceless gift was so badly misused that it proved insufficient and ineffective (1 Timothy 4:2; Titus 1:15). As a result, there arose a need for a revelation such as that contained in the Holy Scriptures that lives and remains forever (1 Peter 1:23).

So, it came to be that some two millennia after creation, God called Abraham away from the idolatry of his house (Genesis 12:1) and made him the father of a people that He would call Israel. This people would become the repository for the revealed Law of God which was written down (Romans 3:2). As a nation, Israel would be separated from other nations and would be dedicated to learn and fulfill all of the words of this Law (Deuteronomy 31:9). Later on, the entire Canon, both Old and new Testaments, would be compiled by holy men under divine inspiration (1 Peter 1:21).

Some forty different authors over a period of over a thousand years wrote under the absolute inspiration of God. The incomparable unity of the Bible, in spite of the significant interval of time and diversity of authors, is one of the undeniable indicators of divine inspiration. Information from different countries and compiled over one and a half millennia, aligning perfectly to complete a magnificently designed structure, proves the existence of a master plan and perfect architect.

This is the case with the Bible. As the revelation of God, the Scriptures declare the will of God to man. The Apostle Peter, when he was an old man, wrote to believers stressing the foundation on which the Christian faith rests (2 Peter 1:16-21). His position is that God had clearly revealed Himself in Christ. Peter wrote that epistle to establish the reality of this act. He affirms that he himself was an eyewitness of the glorious majesty of Christ. The honesty and integrity of the Apostle is worthy of confidence, as is the witness of more than 500 who saw Christ after his resurrection. Peter refers to the occasion when he, James, and John went up the mountain with Christ. There the Lord was transfigured before them and they saw Elijah and Moses speaking with Him. More spectacular than previous appearances were the powerful voice that echoed from the glory of heaven saying: "This is my beloved Son, with whom I am well pleased" (Matthew 17:5).

Therefore, we understand that portions of the Holy word of God were written by eyewitnesses of those things that were to be preserved for the benefit of people today. This is particularly true of the Gospels and book of Acts. We are confident that, in compiling what they had seen and heard, the writers were clearly under the inspiration of the Holy Spirit and wrote without error.

Not only are the Scriptures verifiable by the testimony of eyewitnesses, they are also affirmed by prophecy. Peter wrote that: "We also have the prophetic message as something completely reliable" (2 Peter 1:19), even more so than that of the eyewitnesses. According to Peter there is nothing more convincing than the amazing glory of Christ at the Transfiguration and the majestic voice of the Father speaking from the cloud. However, he also acknowledges that, for those who did not have the privilege of being eyewitnesses, the prophetic word would be a greater proof. Men could say that the eyewitnesses were emotionally overcome and did not really see what they claimed. When prophecy is fulfilled over hundreds of years before both believers and unbelievers, then it becomes undeniable.

Phillip discovered Christ in this manner. He told Nathaniel: "We have found the one Moses wrote about in the Law, and about whom the prophets also wrote – Jesus of Nazareth" (John 1:45 NIV). Later, Phillip instructed the eunuch regarding the prophecy of Isaiah. While teaching His disciples after the resurrection, Jesus said: "This is what I told you while I was still with you: everything must be fulfilled that is written about me in the Law of Moses, the Prophets and the Psalms" (Luke 24:44 NIV).

Following Pentecost and after the first Apostolic miracle, Peter preached to the people saying: "Indeed, beginning with Samuel, all the prophets who have spoken have foretold these days (Acts 3:24 NIV). So, we see that not only were the eyewitness reports important to the writing of the New Testament, but the prophecies of the Old Testament were equally important.

In his effort to exalt the Scriptures as the very Word of God, Peter was careful to note that: "No prophecy of Scripture came about by the prophet's own interpretation of things" (2 Peter 1:20 NIV). That is to say that no prophecy is the result of the prophet's knowledge of the future. We find in 1 Peter 1:10-11 that the prophets spoke of things they themselves could not understand.

The Apostle continued emphasizing that the prophecy did not come about by the will of men, but that holy men of God spoke under the inspiration of the Holy Spirit (2 Peter 1:21). These men were so completely surrendered to God and their inspiration was so absolute, that they wrote the message of God with no errors. The message was the very breath of God and, consequently everything that He wanted it to be. The Scriptures were, therefore, not the result of human impulse or origin, but by inspiration.

The Power of God and With Men[6]

By Antonio Collazo

Then the man said, "Your name will no longer be Jacob, but Israel, because you have struggled with God and with humans and have overcome."... So, Jacob called the place Peniel, saying, "It is because I saw God face to face, and yet my life was spared"Genesis 32:28, 30 (NIV).

WHEN WE SPEAK OF POWER, we refer to the ability to act, or the capacity for action and production; exercising control or being vested with power; having the strength to overcome any resistance. This force must be given to man by a force greater than himself. That is even more valuable for man as he must prove that he is worthy to receive such power.

The words of the referenced text are exciting. God told Jacob: "You have power with God and with men." What more could one desire? If a man has power with God and consequently with men, the means for every kind of success he desires are within his reach. This is the power that the church needs today to accomplish its assigned task.

I want us to clearly understand how this power can be received. We need to seek a worldwide revival of the old-time power that belongs to the children of God. The first

---

[6] Antonio Collazo, "Poder de Dios Y Con Los Hombres," *El Evangelio*, September 2011, 4–5.

step toward this ability to serve should be toward the very fountain of power.

Before we can have power with men, we need to acquire power from God. This is a very important step filled with expectations. I am of the opinion that God wants us to have the ability and capacity to act before He gives us power with authority. Having authority without the capacity to act would impede the cause of Christ.

However, I am afraid that many who take authority are merely putting on an act. This has wounded the faith of many and has resulted in inactivity among the ranks of Christianity to the extent that is has become a weakness.

It is true that the early church was imbued with power on the Day of Pentecost while they prayed in the upper room. However, it is also true that there was an earlier upper room experience. I refer to the last supper with the Lord before the crucifixion. It was there that the Lord prayed for sanctification, announced the betrayal and forced everyone present to do a self-examination. Each one asked: "Is it I, Lord?"

When the Lord sent the disciples to prepare the upper room he said: "And prepare the meal there." Without this first upper room there would never have been the upper room of Pentecost. They went to the Garden of Gethsemane, the Court, Calvary and the empty tomb from that first upper room. Forty days after the resurrection they walked to Bethany with the Lord on His journey toward the ascension. It was here, while preparing to ascend, that He raised

His hands and gave them His final earthly instruction: "Return to Jerusalem until you are filled with power from on high."

And then he was taken out of their sight and they returned to Jerusalem rejoicing. They all went into the upper room according to the instruction of the Lord. This was their first step toward Pentecost and power. This promised power was the anointing of the Holy Spirit that Jesus had said He would send to console, guide, and teach them. He promised that they would receive power after the Holy Spirit came upon them. So, they remained there for several days praying and waiting for the anointing.

When the Day of Pentecost had fully come, they were all in one accord. The Holy Spirit filled the house where they were seated, and they were all filled with power. They were energized with the power of the Holy Spirit and equipped for service.

It was as a result of this anointing that Peter told the cripple at the gate of the Temple: "What I do have I give to you" (Acts 3:6 NIV). The church had power and each individual was anointed. Jesus had said that the Holy Spirit "would be with you forever" (John 14:16 NIV). This explains the powerful operation of the early church and its outstanding success.

Wherever the ministry of the early church reached, there was evidence that it was in touch with God. This is the only means for the effective ministry of the church today as in the past. There is no other means by which the provision of God is possible. The Holy Spirit administers the blessings of God in this dispensation and is the only agent through which God works.

Each church and individual must determine that the Holy Spirit have complete freedom in their life and effort. That is why Paul warns the church at Thessalonica: "Do not quench the Spirit" (1 Thessalonians 5:19). He asked the disciples of John in Ephesus: "Did you receive the Holy Spirit when you believed?" (Acts 19:2 NIV).

It was a Holy Spirit filled man who visited Saul (later Paul) in his distress when he found himself blind after his encounter with the Lord on the road to Damascus. Ananias said to Saul: "Brother Saul, the Lord—Jesus, who appeared to you on the road as you were coming here—has sent me so that you may see again and be filled with the Holy Spirit" (Acts 9:17 NIV). When he laid his hands on Saul, he received his sight. Scabs fell from his eyes and he was also filled with the Holy Spirit.

Ananias could minister to Saul because he had power with God and with men. He helped him find salvation in spite of the significant human authority with which Saul was invested to act against Ananias and the other Christians.

Both the cases of Ananias with Saul and Peter with Cornelius serve as ideal examples that prove how God uses men who exercise power with Him and with other men for the salvation of sinners and for accomplishing the mission of the church in the world. Ananias and Peter were persons who actually used the terrace or housetop as an altar when they were called by God to accomplish special tasks.

Both were in touch with God and filled with the Holy Spirit. No useful purpose would have been served to send a spiritually weak and deficient person to help Saul or an indecisive person to help Cornelius and his family when they gathered to receive the Holy Spirit. The meeting at the house of Cornelius would not have been anything special without the Power to bring a special blessing.

But this was not the case. Peter went to Cornelius and those gathered with him, the first Gentile congregation that he encountered, with enough power to produce such worship in the meeting, that those who heard him were baptized in the Holy Spirit even as he preached.

The same can be said of Ananias. His prayer restored sight to Saul, who received sufficient power from of high to be transformed into one of the greatest and most powerful ministers the world has ever known.

This is the power of God. The men and women of the early church did not acquire this power through a course of study or by some intellectual achievement. It required a complete transformation of the individual such as could not be provided by any human instrument or institution.

The anointing is so great that the person must be fully surrendered and consecrated to the will and purpose of God. They come to the place where they want to serve others and are willing to sacrifice in order to bless them. That is the reason why many members and leaders of the early church gave their lives as martyrs.

Consider with me the case of Peter and John as they were being prosecuted by the religious leaders. "When they saw the courage of Peter and John and realized that they were unschooled, ordinary men, they were astonished, and they took note that these men had been with Jesus. However, since they could see the man who had been healed standing there with them, there was nothing they could say" (Acts 4:13-14 NIV).

It is possible that Peter and John did not know the answers to the technical questions put to them, which led the religious leaders to conclude that they were common unschooled men. However, they recognized that these men had been with Jesus. They possessed a greater understanding that came from God which they shared with the experts.

These two men had something that they were not ashamed to make known. They had enough faith to share with others, and enough power to exercise it. They had the power of God! They had been filled with the Holy Spirit in the upper room on the Day of Pentecost.

In summary, we end where we first began. This is the power that the church needs today in order to accomplish the task with which it has been entrusted.

The Virgin Birth of Christ[7]

By Antonio Collazo

We believe: "That Jesus Christ is the only begotten Son of the Father, conceived of the Holy Ghost, and born of the Virgin Mary. That Jesus was crucified, buried, and raised from the dead. That He ascended to heaven and is today at the right hand of the Father as the Intercessor" (Church of God Declaration of Faith, article 3).

Although we refer to this third article of our Declaration of Faith as "The virgin birth of Christ", the truth expressed here is far more comprehensive. It expresses our absolute and complete belief in all that Christ was, is, and will be for us. Clearly, the virgin birth is the key event that identifies Christ with the Old Testament prophecies of a Redeemer from Genesis 3:15 through Malachi 4. It validates the statements made by Saint John in the first chapter of his Gospel where he says: "In the beginning was the Word, and the Word was with God, and the Word was God...The Word became flesh and made his dwelling among us. We have seen his glory, the glory of the one and only Son, who came from the Father, full of grace and truth" (John 1:1, 14 NIV).

There are countless declarations, as much by the Biblical writers as by Christ Himself that are based and animated by the truth of the virgin birth. Let us then, analyze

---

[7] Antonio Collazo, "El Nacimiento Virginal de Cristo," *El Evangelio*, 1982.

this extraordinarily transcendent and miraculous event in light of the Holy Scriptures.

The first book of the Bible contains a prophecy about the virgin birth of Christ. We hear the following prophetic words in the Garden of Eden that offer a promise of redemption to the fallen Adam and to the entire human race: "And I will put enmity between you and the woman, and between your offspring and hers" (Genesis 3:15 NIV). Jesus is called the seed of a woman. There is no other man in human history of whom it was said that he was the seed of a woman. Repeatedly, we read in the Word of God about the seed of Abraham and the seed of man, but the seed of woman is a unique concept where the newborn child can be understood to be the result of a virgin birth.

The virgin birth was also prophesized by Jeremiah: "For the LORD has created a new thing in the earth—a woman shall encompass a man" (Jeremiah 31:22 NKJV). This means that a woman alone, without being joined to a man, will give birth to a son. This passage of Scripture contains the promise of a miraculous virgin birth. Consider another of many significant prophecies: "Therefore the Lord himself will give you a sign: The virgin will conceive and give birth to a son and will call him Immanuel" (Isaiah 7:14 NIV). The fulfillment of this prophecy is recorded in the Gospel of Matthew: "She will give birth to a son, and you are to give him the name Jesus, because he will save his people from their sins." All this took place to fulfill what the Lord had said through the prophet: "The virgin will conceive and give birth to a son, and they will call him

Immanuel" (which means "God with us"). (Matthew 1:21-23 NIV).

Some modern translators and critics try to create a cloud of doubt about the virgin birth by substituting the term young woman for virgin. This is simply another ruse of Satan to eliminate the doctrine of the virgin birth, which would be a sign to the Hebrew nation. The fact that a young woman would become a mother does not constitute a sign for anyone. This happens with millions of women every day. The sign had to be something extraordinary to serve as evidence of the fulfillment of a covenant of God. This birth had to result in such a holy one as to be called Immanuel, which means God with us. He was God manifest in the flesh (John 1:14).

The miraculous preservation of the messianic line is another conclusive proof of the virgin birth of Christ. Many consider the genealogy of Christ in the first chapters of Matthew and Luke as simply a list of names without any particular significance. However, these two lists represent a genealogy of forty-two generations from Christ back to Abraham, a period of nearly two thousand years. The registry begins in Matthew 1:1: "This is the genealogy of Jesus the Messiah the son of David, the son of Abraham:" (NIV). Consider the promise of God to Abraham. "I will bless those who bless you, and whoever curses you I will curse; and all peoples on earth will be blessed through you" (Genesis 12:3 NIV). Some years later Jacob, a grandson of Abraham, told his son Judah that a ruler of Israel would come from his lineage. "The scepter will not depart from Judah, nor the ruler's staff from between his feet, until he to whom it belongs shall come and the obedience of the nations shall be his" (Genesis 49:10 NIV). The promises of God were marvelously fulfilled. From the time of Abraham until the birth of Christ at least one son from each generation grew to adulthood to have sons of his own. In this way there was an uninterrupted succession of male descendants so that our Lord would be heir to the throne of David. The work of the Holy Spirit is clearly apparent in the genealogy of Matthew chapter 1.

Thirty-nine times in the listing the Holy Spirit used the term "begat", but in verse 16 the language changed. "And Jacob begat Joseph the husband of Mary, of whom was born Jesus, who is called Christ" (Matthew 1:16 KJV). The Scripture does not say that Joseph begat Jesus, but rather that Jesus was born of Mary. It was in this way that the entry of Jesus into the world was a supernatural event.

Nowhere in Scripture does Joseph claim to be the father of Jesus. From a legal standpoint Jesus was his son and was seen as such by the community. At one point they asked, "Isn't this the carpenter's son?" (Matthew 13:55 NIV); and again, "Isn't this Joseph's son?" (Luke 4:22 NIV). The account of His baptism records: "Now Jesus himself was about thirty years old when he began his ministry. He was the son, so it was thought, of Joseph" (Luke 3:23 NIV). Joseph never claimed Jesus as his son, and Jesus refused to acknowledge Joseph as his father. When Mary and Joseph had left him behind in Jerusalem they returned to find him in the temple asking and answering questions with the doctors of the Law. "When his parents saw him, they were astonished. His mother said to him, 'Son, why have you treated us like this? Your father and I have been anxiously searching for you.' 'Why were you searching for me?' he asked. 'Didn't you know I had to be in my Father's house?'" (Luke 2:48,49 NIV). It is as if He had said: "Joseph's business is that of a carpenter, but my Father's business is the salvation of the world."

The specificity of the Holy Spirit's instruction to Joseph to flee to Egypt is amazing. Not once did the Spirit refer to Jesus as the son of Joseph. "Get up," he said, "Take the child and his mother" (Matthew 2:13 NIV). This phrase appears at least four times. Later, God Himself claims the child as His own when He said: "Out of Egypt I called my son" (Matthew 2:15 NIV).

Another conclusive proof of the virgin birth is the testimony of the angels. Gabriel approached Mary and said, "Greetings, you who are highly favored! The Lord is with you." Mary was greatly troubled at his words and wondered what kind of greeting this might be. However, the angel said to her, "Do not be afraid, Mary; you have found favor with God. You will conceive and give birth to a son, and you are to call him Jesus. He will be great and will be called the Son of the Most High. The Lord God will give him the throne of his father David" (Luke 1:28-32 NIV). Her response was understandable. "How will this be," Mary asked the angel, "since I am a virgin?" (Luke 1:34 NIV). She questioned the biological possibility that an unmarried virgin could become a mother. However, the angel said: "The Holy Spirit will come on you, and the power of the Most High will overshadow you. So, the holy one to be born will be called the Son of God" (Luke 1:35 NIV). Herein the mystery of the virgin birth is revealed. This miracle came about through the direct operation of the power of the Holy Spirit.

Those critics who insist on classifying Jesus Christ as the result of a promiscuous union would do well to give attention to the declaration: "So the holy one to be born will be called the Son of God" (Luke 1:35 NIV). They should pay close attention to the Biblical declaration that Mary was a virgin and Joseph was just man. If there still remains a thread of doubt in their mind as to the possibility of a miracle of God, they should note that "For with God nothing will be impossible" (Luke 1:37 NIV). Note that this passage is not a general statement but is made specifically with reference to the virgin birth. It was God Himself who formed the body of the Lord Jesus Christ.

The many miracles surrounding His birth are irrefutable evidence that he was born of a virgin. Additionally, the angel of the Lord also predicted that His mission was to be the Savior of the world. Micah the prophet wrote that Bethlehem would be the place of His birth (Micah 5:2). The hymn sung by the angelic choir announcing the birth and the appearance of the star in the heavens were also supernatural manifestations that surrounded His birth. With so many extraordinary events accompanying His birth, why then would it seem unbelievable that Jesus Himself was a miracle?

The virgin birth of Christ was essential for the purpose of providing a Redeemer for all of humanity. By means of the virgin birth Jesus became the incarnate Son of God, which is to say that He was Deity clothed in human flesh. He was God and, at the same time, a perfect human without sin. Had He not been born of a virgin he would have been an ordinary human with a sinful and corrupt nature, disqualified from being our Redeemer. If this were so, Christ would not have been able to accomplish the work of redemption and we would be dead in our sins.

His purpose in coming into the world was clear: "He will save his people from their sins" (Matthew 1:21 NIV). Luke wrote: "Today in the town of David a Savior has been born to you; he is the Messiah, the Lord" (Luke 2:11 NIV). Paul also wrote: "Christ Jesus came into the world to save sinners" (1Timothy 1:15 NIV); and again declared: "God sent his Son, born of a woman, born under the law, to redeem those under the law" (Galatians 4:4-5 NIV).

Only a Son born of a virgin could satisfy all of the requirements to secure our salvation. First: He had to be pure, without sin. Without the virgin birth, He would have been born in sin. The Bible clearly states: "Therefore, just as sin entered the world through one man, and death through sin, and in this way death came to all people, because all sinned" (Romans 5:12 NIV). Since Adam, every person is sinful by nature. Christ testifies to his own impeccability when, standing before the multitude, He declared: "Can any of you prove me guilty of sin?" (John 8:46 NIV). On three occasions, Pilate declared: "I find no fault in him" (John 18:38; 19:4,6 KJV). Pilate's wife said: "Have thou nothing to do with that just man" (Matthew 27:19 KJV). Judas said: "I have sinned in that I have betrayed the innocent blood" (Matthew 27:4 KJV). Peter wrote: "He committed no sin, and no deceit was found in his mouth" (1 Peter 2:22 NIV).

Second: His blood had to be incorruptible because, had it been tainted by sin, the sacrifice at Calvary would have been in vain. The Bible is clear: "For you know that it was not with perishable things such as silver or gold that you were redeemed from the empty way of life handed down to you from your ancestors, but with the precious blood of Christ, a lamb without blemish or defect" (1 Peter 1:18, 19 NIV).

Finally: The Redeemer had to be at once both fully God and fully human. In other words, He had to be a God-Man. Having been born of a virgin, Jesus was both. He was the only begotten Son of the Father, and also the son of Mary. He could reach and touch the heart of God through His human nature, and thus bring humanity to be reconciled to the Father. "All this is from God, who reconciled us to himself through Christ and gave us the ministry of reconciliation:" (2 Corinthians 5:18 NIV).

Sermons

In addition to sharing articles by Reverend Collazo published in *El Evangelio* as included above, I want to share some of his sermon outlines. These were provided by his daughter, Pérsida (Tita) Collazo Pagán from notebooks of sermons that have been preserved. They demonstrate the pastoral and didactic care that he gave in their preparation to minister to his audience.

Bless the Lord, O My Soul[8]

January 2, 1968

"Bless the LORD, O my soul; And all that is within me, *bless* His holy name!" (Psalm 103:1 NKJV).

"Who forgives all your iniquities, Who heals all your diseases, Who redeems your life from destruction, Who crowns you with lovingkindness and tender mercies, Who satisfies your mouth with good *things, So that* your youth is renewed like the eagle's" (Psalm 103:3-5 NKJV).

Introduction: A conversation with himself

- Compare this dialogue with that of the rich man in the parable.

    "Bless the Lord, O my soul" (Psalm 103:1 NKJV).

    "Soul, you have many goods" (Luke 12:19 NKJV).

- We often talk to ourselves and a recording could reveal;

    The words of a fool

    The words of wisdom

1. Follow the words of the Psalmist: "And forget not all His benefits:" (Psalm 103:2 NKJV).

    o Consider the many personal reasons to give thanks (vv. 3-5)

        ▪ Forgiveness of sins

---

[8] Antonio Collazo, "Bendice Alma Mía a Jehová," January 1968, Sermon notebook of Antonio Collazo.

- Healing
- Life redeemed from destruction
- God's love given to the brethren
- Renewed strength

"I will sing to the LORD as long as I live; I will sing praise to my God while I have my being" (Psalm 104:33 NKJV).

2. Remembering reasons from the past
   o Showed His way to Moses
   o Showed His works to the children of Israel throughout their history

The Psalmist determines to remember to "Bless the Lord."

3. Meditating, he offers blessings to the Lord: Psalm 104
   o Blesses the Lord for His greatness, honor, and majesty (Psalm 104:1 NKJV).
   o Sees the Power and Providence of God in seven wonders
     - The heavens vs. 2
     - The earth vs. 5
     - The waters vs. 6
     - The vegetation vs. 14
     - The moon vs. 19
     - The sun vs. 19
     - The sea vs. 25

4. The response of the soul:
   o Psalm 104:33 "I will sing to the LORD as long as I live; I will sing praise to my God while I have my being" (NKJV).

- o "The LORD *is* merciful and gracious, Slow to anger, and abounding in mercy" (Psalm 103:8 NKJV).
- o "Bless the LORD, you His angels, Who excel in strength, who do His word, Heeding the voice of His word. Bless the LORD, all *you* His hosts, *You* ministers of His, who do His pleasure. Bless the LORD, all His works, In all places of His dominion. Bless the LORD, O my soul! (Psalm 103:20-22 NKJV).

5. All my being:
   - o "And all that is within me, *bless* His holy name!" (Psalm 103:1 NKJV).
     - ▪ Something more than memory and the mind. These are expressions of praise. They emanate from the heart. The essence of the Psalm includes the emotions of the heart. It is uplifted by the mercies of God.
       - • Exalted to the point that it invites the angels and angelic hosts to join in praise. (vv.20-22)
       - • We see Him in the rising of the sun, the song of the birds, the fragrance of the roses, the sea.

Prepared for a Great Encounter[9]
1 Samuel 17:28-37

January 9, 1958

I. David was facing an unexpected situation
    o He knew where he was going, but did not know what he was going to encounter – sometimes this is also true of us
    o He is aware of the hopeless circumstance of the army, and determines that he himself will face the giant Goliath
    o He has won victories in the past
        ▪ The assurance of victory depends in part with how we face the conflict. If you have been careless in minor endeavors, you will fail if you maintain the same attitude. If you come wearing the medals earned in the midst of battle with a shout of victory, that sets another tone altogether
II. Consider the trophies won by David before confronting the giant

> "Why did you come down here? And with whom have you left those few sheep in the wilderness? I know your pride and the insolence of your heart, for you have

---

[9] Antonio Collazo, "Bendice Alma Mía a Jehová," January 1958, Sermon notebook of Antonio Collazo.

come down to see the battle." And David
said, "What have I done now? *Is there* not
a cause?" (1 Samuel 17:28-29 NKJV).

o *He had conquered his temper.* Note Eliab's annoyed reaction on seeing him, and the young
champion's calm response. This control served
him well when he took aim at the giant with his
slingshot. Uncontrolled emotion or anger af-
fects the clarity of our vision and the stability
of our hands

o *He had conquered fear.* "Let no man's heart fail
because of him; your servant will go and fight
with this Philistine" (vs. 32)
  ▪ There was no panic, uncertainty, or de-
    bilitating emotion. He trusted in God
    and won the victory. Now in light of his
    previous victories, with his confidence
    squarely placed in God, he advances to
    face Goliath
  ▪ There were no excited shouts to mask
    the fear or to raise enthusiasm. He
    spoke and was perfectly calm – be-
    cause he had conquered fear

o *He had conquered unbelief.* He learned to believe in and to depend on God
  ▪ His confidence was not affected by the
    shadows or dark clouds. It was now
    clear and calm based on his own expe-
    rience of the PROVIDENTIAL CARE of
    God in the past

- He had personally experienced the POWER of God in the face of the lion and the bear.

The Blood of Jesus Christ[10]
January 14, 1968

"But if we walk in the light as He is in the light, we have fellowship with one another, and the blood of Jesus Christ His Son cleanses us from all sin" (1 John 1:7 NKJV).

I. The fisherman and his catch
- o Set out to fish
- o Pulled up his nets
- o Returned to shore
- o His catch on that day was priceless
  - It cost the death of His Son

II. The experience of evangelist Charles Finney
- o His crusade and text – 1 John 1:7
- o The Guest – the deacons
- o Invitation to Finney
- o Account of the Visitor
  - His story
- o Finney: the blood of Jesus, etc.

III. The experience of the following night

IV. Conclusion

---

[10] Antonio Collazo, "La Sangre de Cristo Jesús," January 1968, Sermon notebook of Antonio Collazo

Press Ahead From Here[11]
Philippians 3:13-16

Brethren, I do not count myself to have apprehended; but one thing *I do,* forgetting those things which are behind and reaching forward to those things which are ahead, I press toward the goal for the prize of the upward call of God in Christ Jesus. Therefore, let us, as many as are mature, have this mind; and if in anything you think otherwise, God will reveal even this to you. Nevertheless, to *the degree* that we have already attained, let us walk by the same rule, let us be of the same mind (NKJV).

I. We press ahead, but have not yet arrived
    o The end of each year signals a stopping point to *review,* and a departure point to *press ahead*
        ▪ Academic year
        ▪ Business year
        ▪ Governmental year
        ▪ Biological year
II. Press ahead in the truth
III. Press ahead in brotherhood – companionship
    o What kind of friend have you been?
IV. Press ahead in service
    o How have you been of service in the past year?
V. Press ahead in WORSHIP – DEVOTION – PRAISE

---

[11] Antonio Collazo, "Avanza Desde Aquí," n.d., Sermon notebook of Antonio Collazo.

     o Remember that although you have advanced, you have not yet arrived

VI. Illustration

The Torn Veil[12]
Mark 15:38
"Then the veil of the temple was torn in two from top to bottom" (NKJV).

I. Signified an ending
- o The end of symbolism
  - ▪ The tabernacle
  - ▪ Priestly vestments
  - ▪ Animal sacrifice
- o The end of the dominion of sin
  - ▪ Up until Christ, sin prevailed
  - ▪ The Son lived free from sin
- o The end of the priesthood
  - ▪ Role as intercessor
- o The end of separation
  - ▪ Expulsion from the garden
  - ▪ I am the gate

II. Signified new life
- o Life as an altar
  - ▪ "For I am now ready to be offered" (2 Timothy 4:6 KJV).
- o Life as a journey
  - ▪ "The time of my departure is at hand" (2 Timothy 4:6 KJV).
- o Life as a battle

---

[12] Antonio Collazo, "El Velo Roto," n.d., Sermon notebook of Antonio Collazo.

- ▪ "I have fought the good fight" (2 Timothy 4:7 NKJV).
  - o Life as a race
    - ▪ "I have finished the race" (2 Timothy 4:7 NKJV).
  - o Life as assurance
    - ▪ "I have kept the faith" (2 Timothy 4:7 NKJV).
    - ▪ "I am the way" (John 14:6 KJV).
    - ▪ "You delight in truth…" (Psalm 51:6 ESV).
    - ▪ A contrast. "You are of *your* father the devil…He was a murderer from the beginning, and does not stand in the truth, because there is no truth in him" (John 8:44 NKJV).

III. The living Word
  - o His truth speaks for us when we surrender to Him
  - o "He only *is* my rock and my salvation" (Psalm 62:2 NKJV).
  - o "He is my defense; I shall not be greatly moved" (Psalm 62:2 NKJV).
  - o The whole armor of God – Ephesians 6
    - ▪ Girded with truth – "I am the truth" (John 14:6 KJV).
      - • Delight in truth – Psalm 51:6
      - • "that you may be sincere and without offense" (Philippians 1:10 NKJV).
    - ▪ Breastplate of righteousness – "But of Him you are in Christ Jesus, who

became for us wisdom from God— and righteousness" (1 Corinthians 1:30 NKJV).

- The righteousness of God the first outcome of the death of Christ. Through His death comes righteousness
- Shoes of the Gospel of peace
  - "For He Himself is our peace' (Ephesians 2:14 NKJV).
  - Soldier equipped with proper footwear for battle
- Shield of faith
  - Faith in Christ is the fountain and resource of life
- Helmet of salvation
  - "He only *is* my rock and my salvation" (Psalm 62:2 NKJV).
  - Sword of the Spirit
  - "And the Word became flesh...full of grace and truth" (John 1:14 NKJV).

Rejoicing for the Afflicted[13]
John 16:33

"These things I have spoken to you, that in Me you may have peace. In the world you will have tribulation; but be of good cheer, I have overcome the world" (John 16:33 NKJV).

I. Place of testing – "In the world"
II. Secret for the victory – "I have overcome"
III. Words of comfort – "Be of good cheer"

A Great Responsibility
Galatians 6:7

"Do not be deceived, God is not mocked; for whatever a man sows, that he will also reap. Do not be deceived, God is not mocked; for whatever a man sows, that he will also reap"
(Galatians 6:7 NKJV).

I. Great responsibility – "whatever a man sows"
II. Unchangeable law – "that will he also reap"
III. Unalterable fact – "God cannot be mocked
IV. Warning – "Do not be deceived"
    a. "Behold, I stand at the door and knock. If anyone hears My voice and opens the door, I will come in to him and dine with him, and he with Me" (Revelation 3:20 NKJV).

---

[13] Antonio Collazo, "Regocijo Para El Atribulado," n.d., Sermon notebook of Antonio Collazo.

Chapter 9

The Husband, Father, Relative, Pastor, Overseer, and Friend

Vivid recollection by Ligia Collazo-Douglas of her dear father[1]

Daddy was a saint, a very calm and easy-going man. I remember him treating us with much tenderness. He expressed his love for us in concrete actions, not just words. Of course, it is important to understand that his generation grew up in homes where there were not many verbal expressions of love. In his time such expressions like "I love you" were not often spoken by his parents. So those words were not part of his vocabulary, but his actions spoke volumes. In spite of the fact that most of his time was taken up pastoring the church at the Parada 22 in Santurce and the supervision of the Church of God *Mission Board* in Puerto Rico, he always found time on Saturdays to take us to the Luis Muñoz Rivera Park in San Juan. On many Saturday nights he took us to Old San Juan. There I

---

[1] Ligia Collazo Douglas, interview by Wilfredo Estrada-Adorno, August 2017.

remember seeing the store windows like the one at González Padin. We could only see them from the sidewalk as the stores were already closed. Still, it was quite a spectacle.

Ligia describes an unforgettable experience that demonstrated the patience and kindness of her dad. She recounted that she was to graduate from 9th grade, as a young lady feeling the peer pressure of her classmates to cut her hair. Naturally, if the daughter of the pastor of the leading church and overseer of the denomination were to cut her hair, it would be a scandal of major proportion in

Puerto Rico. However, she tells that, with the help of her mother, and against the wishes of her father, she went and did it. "After I cut my hair I thought that my father would punish me severely since I had disobeyed his instruction." On her way home from the beauty shop she ran into her father near his office, and he followed her all the way home and asked, "Did you cut your hair?" Ligia says her response was a timid "yes" as she quickly headed up the stairs to their home on the second floor of the church building. She realized that Brother Tony was right behind her and said, "The remaining time you are here you will need to wear a kerchief on your head to attend church." She remembered that it would be two weeks because, following her graduation, she would leave for New York to live with her grandparents Brother and Sister Lugo to continue her education there. What she remembers most warmly about that experience was that her father did not punish her or show impatience with her in spite of her disobedience. "That response from my dad showed me the quality of love that he expressed to us all."

Reflections from his only son, Juan Antonio (Totoño) Collazo-Lugo[2]

I have been singularly blessed in my life to have had a grandfather and father who were exemplary figures in my life. However, I was a restless youth who created many problems for my dad. It was easy for me to get into trouble, but my father never gave up on me. I remember that he took me with him when he would go out to preach. He could not leave me with my sisters because I would get into fights with them. If my mother told him about it, he would punish me and say, "You can never raise your hand to strike a woman." So, I often accompanied him to the churches across the Island. There was a sermon of his that I will never forget. It told about the many "hats" that Jesus wore. He said: Jesus saved, healed, loved, and forgave. On another occasion I heard dad preach a message that referred to the images in the stained glass windows of the church. He said; "Here is Jesus as the way, here is Jesus demonstrating His love, and here He is the Good Shepherd." I was impressed by the explanation and actually stayed for the entire sermon. Usually, while he preached,

---

[2] Juan Antonio Collazo Lugo Collazo, interview by Wilfredo Estrada-Adorno, August 2017.

The Husband...

I would sneak out of the service, but he captured my attention on that night. I remember that he said: "Time will not permit me to finish the sermon tonight, but I will complete it the next time I come." Sadly, I never heard the rest of the sermon as I did not accompany him on his return.

My heart is saddened because I later left the church and lived a life separated from the Lord. On one occasion, while I was stationed in France as a member of the US Armed Forces, my father and grandfather (Reverend Juan L. Lugo) visited me. It was an amazing encounter. They had been traveling on a special tour of the Holy Land and stopped over in France to see me on their way back home. I never dreamed that I would so happy to see my dad as I was then. Memories of my childhood immediately bubbled up in my mind. Visiting the Luis Muñoz Rivera Park, and the walks on the streets of San Juan, Puerto Rico, and the Bronx and Manhattan in New York. Dad loved to walk. Those memories in France, now as adult separated from the Lord caused me to reconsider. I never heard my father tell me how much he loved me, but always, always, whenever he would leave he would tell me: "Totoño never forget that I continue to pray for you, I keep praying for you." I have no doubt that those prayers played a key role in my return to the feet of the Master! That is something I will never forget!

Memories from his daughter Pérsida (Tita) Collazo-Pagán[3]

My memory of my father is that he was both a gentle and strict person; he was a man who liked things to be well done. However, he was not a person that would get worked up over small things. He did not go around yelling or speaking loudly, but rather spoke in a moderate way. Sometimes mom would tell him something and he would say: "Yes Pérsida, you are right, ok." I never heard him argue with my mother.

Sometimes when he was in the pulpit I thought that he sounded more like a Baptist preacher because he had a deliberate style and did not yell. Also, I never heard him speak in tongues. He told us that he spoke in tongues when he was baptized in the Holy Spirit, but after that, never again. Clearly, he was filled with the Holy Spirit as was evident by his life and the way he lived it.

As a little girl I remember that he would lie down on the sofa at our house, and because he had straight hair, we sisters, especially Raquel, Tata, and myself would play with it and put little bows and clasps in it. Back then we liked for him to lie on the sofa because coins would fall out of his pockets when we combed his hair and we would collect them. I also remember that there was no service at the church on Saturdays. He would take us to San Juan to walk by the stores. He also took us five to the Luis Muñoz

---

[3] Persida Collazo Pagán, interview by Wilfredo Estrada-Adorno, August 2017.

Rivera Park and would sit there and watch the baseball game played at the Sixto Escobar stadium.

Another thing I remember is that he took us to Julián Blanco School every day. We had to cross Fernández Juncos and Juan Ponce de León Streets to get to school. He took us in the mornings and brought us back home at noon for lunch. Then he took us back and came for us in the afternoon. When he was away, he would ask Pérez Sánchez or another member of the church to come for us. Often, we were annoyed because we preferred not having anyone come after us, so we could walk all the way by ourselves. We did it several times when he could not get anyone else and we thoroughly enjoyed the opportunity.

I must say that my father was a very punctual person; he was never late. What most impressed me about my dad is that he lived what he preached. And that is how I remember my beloved father.

Raquel Collazo remembers her father[4]

My dad was very special to me. He was a very calm person, and it seemed as if nothing really upset him. In this sense, I see myself as my father's daughter made of the same "stuff" as him. As Ligia has already said, he was always very tender toward his daughters and son. Today we understand the pressure he felt as the family lived upstairs in the church building. Sometimes our misadventures did

---

[4] Raquel Collazo, interview by Wilfredo Estrada-Adorno, August 2017.

not conform to the high standards that the church members expected.

I never saw my parents argue; if they did, it was never in front of us. Any situation like that was addressed in private, and never publically. I never saw my father mistreat my mother, but always treated her with deference and kindness. He was always a gentleman and an example worth imitating.

Raquel remembers as a child when they lived in Caparra Terrace in Rio Piedras that, when her dad parked the car, she was the one who washed it. "When he came home tired from work he would lie down on the sofa and I combed his hair and shined his shoes. He would be very still while I combed his hair." She also remembers an incident when none of the neighborhood kids would play with a neighbor girl. Raquel told her dad about it and he told her: "Never judge a person by what others say; talk with her to see why the others think about her the way they do. If you feel you need to separate yourself from her too; then do it. However, never act on the basis of what others say." That advice has remained with me throughout my life.

On another occasion, Raquel remembered when her brother, Totoño was about to hit her. Daddy noticed and reprimanded him strongly. "Never raise your hand to assault a woman; not your hand nor your voice." He could speak in that manner because my brother had never seen him raise a hand to strike my mother or any of us girls.

I also remember another conversation when I was a teenager in New York City and thinking about romance. He told me: "You can have all the freedom you want as long as it does not reflect negatively on my ministry." Those words from my dad struck home. I never wanted to do anything that would cause him to be ashamed.

Finally, I want to say that I very much enjoyed my dad as a teacher. In fact, in the last church he pastored in Newburgh, New York, I was the one who took responsibility to drive the vehicle the pick up those who wanted to come to the worship service.

Memories from the youngest daughter, Rebecca (Tata), his "pet"[5]

My heart leaps with joy and love in remembering and thinking about "My Daddy." His gentleness, sweet smile, laugh, and joyful character were just a few of his many virtues.

When we were small, my sisters and I enjoyed playing with his hair while he tried to rest on the sofa. It was special when he drove us in the car to school and picked us up in the afternoon. Some of our friends occasionally took advantage of the "lift." He helped us fill the boxes with grass for the three Wise Men, and later on Epiphany we enjoyed an outing to the beach at Vega Baja with members of the church he pastored at Parada 22. Often after the service we walked to a nearby bakery to buy warm bread. Some Saturdays we went to the Luis Muñoz Rivera

---

[5] A Puerto Rican expression used to identify the youngest child. Rebecca Collazo, interview by Wilfredo Estrada-Adorno, August 2017.

Park in San Juan, and while he enjoyed the baseball game at the nearby Sixto Escobar stadium, we played and ran all over the place. Later we went to look in the store windows in Old San Juan; he, very proudly taking the arm of the beautiful lady God had given him for his wife accompanied by his five "chicks." I, of course, very proud to be his little pet.

His example as a servant of God was beyond reproach. Dedicated to his call, he was a man of integrity, honest, sincere, loyal, generous and fully surrendered. My daddy, Brother Tony as he was affectionately called, was well respected and loved by his parishioners, his neighbors, his colleagues in ministry, and everyone who had the honor of knowing him. Knowing that I will see my Daddy again fills me with much happiness and joy!

A word from Doctor Esdras Betancourt[6]

Bishop Antonio Collazo: A leader with the spirit of Solomon

I met Bishop Antonio Collazo in 1945 when I was ten years old. My father, Ángel Betancourt, was pastor of the Church of God in the Hoare district and Brother Collazo was the national overseer of the Church of God. Our church building burned to the ground and was a total loss. Brother Collazo came to inspect the progress of the reconstruction. It was interesting to see him sitting on the

---

[6] Esdras Betancourt, interview by Wilfredo Estrada-Adorno, May 8, 2017.

beams that were to be the roof reading the comics in the paper and how he laughed.

During that time, he served as the national overseer and pastor of the church at Parada 22 in Santurce, Puerto Rico. That is where the national conventions were held and where I first saw him serve as interpreter for the officials from the International Offices of the Church of God in Cleveland, Tennessee. As a result, he gained attention in that role which is something he considered a gift. For many years following, he served as interpreter for many well-known leaders and evangelists like T. L. Osborn, Oral Roberts, Billy Graham, T. L. Lowery, and others.

The conventions at his church were well attended and each church reported their annual statistics and activities. One thing I remember well is a film that he showed about his trip to Israel. I also remember that he was the only one who had a car that, on occasion, we had to push to get it started.

I did not see overseer Collazo again until 1958. The Spanish work east of the Mississippi had grown and was supervised by Reverend Henry C. Stoppe. The pastors felt it was time to have a Hispanic overseer. At a conference held at the church pastored by Juan L. Lugo at Third Avenue and 116th Street in Manhattan this need was addressed, and Brother Collazo was chosen to serve as Overseer. Most of the churches in the district at that time had been established by pastors who emigrated from Puerto Rico. They had served under the ministry of Brother Tony and, before his arrival, sent their ministerial reports to Puerto Rico.

In March of 1958 I had committed my life to the Lord and received the call to ministry. In the Fall of 1959, Brother Collazo took me and his daughter Ligia to Lee College. After graduating from Lee in 1963 I returned to New York and, two months later, he installed me as pastor of the church at Third Avenue and 100th Street. The day of my installation he said to me: "You will learn many things in this pastorate that will help you throughout your ministry." With the passing of time I have come to see those words as prophetic.

Two years after assuming that pastorate, I was named by the World Missions Department of the Church of God to be a professor at the newly established Bible Seminary in Switzerland. I taught in both English and Spanish, and in the summer visited small Church of God groups in Spain, Portugal, Gibraltar, and the Horn of Africa. What surprised me greatly was that on the day I left for Europe he was at the John F. Kennedy airport, late at night, to see me off.

After two years of service in Europe I decided to return to the United States. When Overseer Collazo learned of my return he asked me to work as his Director of Youth and Christian Education. One of the tasks assigned to me was to establish an evening Bible Institute.

What most impressed me about Brother Tony was his ability to conduct business meetings with pastors. He did so with much wisdom, sensitivity and firmness. He answered tough questions with the wisdom of Solomon, or as if he was a lawyer.

The most surprising thing to me was what he did after he retired. He enrolled in college and earned his degree.

The Husband...

He could have received credit toward his degree for his previous life experience, but he refused. In that, he was an example to all of us. Let us never stop growing in our Christian ministry!

A word from Reverend Ignacio Macías[7]

Reverend Antonio Collazo was my first overseer in Michigan when we were part of the Northeast District. In that period, the District covered everything east of the Mississippi. I had studied by correspondence and, in 1964, was credentialed as an Exhorter and assigned the pastorate of the Church of God in Lansing, Michigan. This was our first pastorate and he filled the role of parent and mentor to my wife Irma and me. I thank God because he taught us much and took us under wing as if we were his own children.

Brother Tony had a gift of dealing with people. I saw him lead business meetings in churches where it seemed that some there were about to come to blows. However, Brother Tony, with a masterful calm allowed everyone to have their say, and with his characteristic patience took control of the meeting. Within 10 to 15 minutes while he addressed the differences with conciliatory grace, the meeting adjourned peacefully. What seemed likely to end a fight, ended with hugs and good will between the attendees. That was Brother Tony.

---

[7] Ignacio Macías, interview by Wilfredo Estrada-Adorno, June 5, 2017.

I learned much from Brother Tony. I know that he was a minister who began at the bottom and worked hard to advance. As a successful pastor in Puerto Rico he guided many young people like Manuel Pérez Sánchez, Héctor Camacho, José Luis Santana, Loida Collazo-Camacho, and many others. Certainly, he had the ability to advise and to speak which contributed to his success. He was part of a generation that lived by faith in the call of God. He was an eloquent preacher who was gifted in speaking the word.

Some thoughts from the patriarch Antonino Bonilla

I had an extraordinary interview with the Reverend Antonino Bonilla[8], apostle of the Church of God in Latin America, where he shared memories of Reverend Antonio Collazo. The following paragraphs contain his reflections.

Brother Collazo reminds me much of an Old Testament prophet. His background as pastor of the church at Parada 22 in Santurce, Puerto Rico gave him an authority as a leader much like those prophets. His church became much like a city of refuge for those who passed by the building, many whom became part of his ministry. That same image of prophet followed him when he came to minister in the United States. In this way, his influence, amiable character, and strong personality helped him establish new churches in New York and neighboring areas among the Puerto Rican diaspora that had come to the United States from the Island.

I must say that you should write a chapter about his ministry as an interpreter. He traveled extensively with evangelist T. L. Osborn throughout Latin America. As a

---

[8] Bonilla interview.

result, he left an extraordinary impression as such translating for various evangelists from the United States. He also had a great relationship with the leaders of the Church of God who appreciated his ability as an interpreter. Then write an inspiring chapter about his work interpreting for the Church of God leaders who were opening up to outreach to Latin America. Brother Tony was the interpreter who accompanied them on these trips.

Felipe Montañez[9], one of his sons in ministry remembers

What follows here are the thoughts of Felipe Montañez, pastor, evangelist, and Church of God missionary to Latin America. Felipe and his wife Rachel have been blessed with a beautiful family and a fruitful and long life. They are currently retired and living in San Antonio, Texas. Felipe remembers his role model and mentor.

There is much to say about Reverend Antonio Collazo, my dear "Brother Tony" and of the work of the Church of God in Puerto Rico. I can tell you about the Pentecostal Church of God, Inc. on America Street in Santurce where a young 28 year-old Brother Tony arrived. He, along with Brother Johnny Pérez, co-pastored that church which was the largest church in Puerto Rico at the time.

Brother Tony played basketball with the youth on a court adjacent to the church. He was a pastor that I always admired. I went many places with him when the work

----

[9] Felipe Montañez, interview by Wilfredo Estrada-Adorno, June 5, 2017.

known as the First Pentecostal Church, Inc. was established in 1940. It was a time when we in the church encountered circumstances that were not right, and our beloved pastor Reverend Juan L. Lugo was poorly treated. Although I was only 9 years old at the time, I was aware of what was happening in the church. In 1940 Brother Tony began a pastorate that lasted until 1958 when he was transferred by the church to New York City.

My memory of Brother Tony now in my old age is of a man dedicated to the work of the Lord who, in his time, did the best he could, according to his strength and capability to advance the cause of the Master. He was an excellent preacher, and I also enjoyed hearing him play the saxophone and clarinet. Surely, he was an outstanding teacher and preacher; a man fully committed to the work of the Lord. Pastor, friend, mentor! That is how I remember Reverend Antonio Collazo, my dear "Brother Tony."

A reflection from Doctor Victor M. Pagán-Lozada[10]

The summer of 1958, pastor José Quiles took a group of young people from his church in Cataño to be baptized in water at the Church of God *Mission Board* on Europa Street in Santurce. I was one of them. At the time, I did not fully understand what it meant to be baptized at the church that was pastored by Antonio Collazo, one of the most influential ministers that Puerto Rico has produced. I must clarify that my most vivid recollection of the service

---

[10] Víctor M. Pagán Lozada, interview by Wilfredo Estrada-Adorno, Agosto 2017.

is that the baptism was done by Manuel Pérez Sánchez, who served as the assistant pastor. Likely, pastor Collazo was busy fulfilling a responsibility related to his other ministerial portfolio as National Overseer of the Church of God *Mission Board* in Puerto Rico.

In September of that year the pastor, known to all of us as Brother Tony, was transferred to New York. Little by little I learned more about him and even spoke to him on some of his trips to Puerto Rico. On my first trip to New York in 1964 I had the opportunity to share time with him close up. Brother Tony did not send anyone to meet us at the airport when we arrived. He came himself. Heading back to the city, I was struck by the number of cars on the road and commented, "My goodness, what a traffic jam!" I will not forget his correction when he said, "I see many cars, but not a traffic jam because all the cars are moving." In less than an hour I had already learned two things about Brother Tony. He demonstrated his humility and heart of service when he himself came to meet us at the airport, and also his good sense of humor that he occasionally displayed.

When he served on the World Missions Board, I was in Cleveland pursuing my ministerial studies at Lee College. One day he surprised me when he came to my home carrying a bag full of corn fritters. My mouth fell open at the surprise of having such an important person in my humble apartment. A while later it closed as I enjoyed those tasty corn fritters. To this day I do not know where he found those corn fritters in Cleveland, Tennessee.

On two occasions my friendship with Brother Tony created some curious situations. When I was about to graduate from Lee he offered me the opportunity to work with him as Youth and Christian Education Director in the Northeast region where he served as overseer. I was honored at the offer, but the two factors that caused me to turn it down were significant. First, I wanted to return to Puerto Rico to continue in ministry, especially teaching at the Bible Institute. Second, I had a moral obligation to honor the commitment I made to World Missions to return to the Island. That was a condition of my receiving the scholarship that made my studies at Lee possible.

From the second experience with Brother Tony, I learned how transparent he was in his decision-making. At that time my wife Ada and I pastored the Church of God *Mission Board* at the Country Club area in Carolina, Puerto Rico. On one of his visits, he shared with me that he opposed the recommendation of the Chair of the World Missions Board that we be sent as missionary-overseer to a country in South America. In his opinion, we should not leave the pastorate at Country Club.

At this point in my life, when I can take more time for reflection and can appreciate more fully the road the Lord has allowed me to traverse, I thank Him for allowing my path to cross with that of a man of such character and ministerial excellence as was Tony Collazo. And for those things, which can only be explained because God works in mysterious ways, my ministerial journey has allowed me to be in places where his fingerprints still remain. For example, in 1978 Ada and I went to pastor the well-known church at Parada 22 which he founded. In 1986 I was named as the second Hispanic, after Brother Tony, to serve on the World Missions Board. In 1988 I went as

The Husband...

Overseer of the North Central Spanish District which he had also supervised before the Northeast region was divided in two. However, one of the most honorable services the Lord has allowed me to perform, similar to Brother Tony, has been to serve as interpreter for preachers from the United States. In that ministry Brother Tony was the master! I, still, remain the student!

Reverend Pascual Robles and his wife Gladys Navas[11] also remember.

The accounts we heard from those who expressed admiration for the family and ministry life, as well as the extraordinary leadership of Reverend Antonio Collazo, a great man of God, had a profound effect on my life and that of my wife. However, those stories paled when we came to know him personally. The person we knew demonstrated by his words and actions his deep commitment to God, enthusiasm, sensitivity, love, fellowship, friendship, dedication, loyalty, faithfulness, understanding, and generosity. We concluded from our personal knowledge of this distinguished minister that what people said about him did not do justice to the totality of the significant and admirable characteristics of this gifted servant of God. Working in ministry under the wise supervision of Brother Collazo impacted our lives greatly as he was the person who gave us the opportunity to enter the pastoral ministry.

Pascual Robles and Gladys Navas, interview by Wilfredo Estrada-Adorno, June 5, 2017.

He was the type of visionary leader who could see the potential in those that he sensed the Holy Spirit was separating for some area of ministry. You did not have to ask Brother Collazo for a ministry opportunity. He knew when it came, who to select, and how to guide the work of the Lord's servant, providing his endorsement, enthusiasm, and friendship.

Reverend Antonio Collazo was a fearless leader who never felt threatened. He was very secure in the position he occupied and of the call of God on his life. He led with a commitment to glorify God. I never heard him speak of his ministry achievements or abilities. I can attest that his lips glorified the God who called him, and, with his saxophone, offered praises to the God who sustained him. He left it to others to speak of his achievements and the many successes in the trajectory of his ministry.

As an overseer, giving respect to all that I have had in my 51 years of pastoral ministry, Reverend Collazo occupies a place beyond comparison. I always sensed his pastoral care, wise counsel, help at all times, and in every situation. His unexpected visits to our church, he did not need an invitation, were a highlight of our ministry. He would come to the service to hear the preaching. I must relate the wonderful feeling my wife and I shared when he told me that he wanted us to be the pastors for his family. What a great privilege! It was a great honor to pastor the Collazo-Lugo family as well as the Pentecostal pioneer to Puerto Rico, Reverend Juan L. Lugo and his wife Sister Isabelita Ortiz-Lugo. She was an extraordinary teacher of Sacred Scripture. On a separate note, it was Brother Collazo who helped us secure a credit account at the local Sears store in Newburgh, New York using his own credit that we retain to this day.

I cannot overlook how he carried out his ministerial responsibilities when covering the Eastern Spanish District east of the Mississippi, and later, the South Central Spanish District. These were enormous geographical areas that necessitated his being away from home and office for weeks at a time leaving his beloved and tireless wife, Sister Pérsida, to care for the children and other family. I never heard him complain about the challenges of his many responsibilities in ministry. Today I can attest that his entire family remains faithful to the Lord.

His sense of humor is also something I want to mention. Whether by car or plane, traveling with him was an enjoyable experience. He was always jokingly "buying" very expensive things while offering little money. (One example: sometimes while driving along he would say: "look they are selling 25 acres of land; I will offer $20.00. What do you think?") Aboard a plane the flight attendants laughed with him over the gibberish he taught them in Spanish.

One thing that Brother Tony easily gained was the respect and admiration of those with whom he worked. He was very respectful, friendly, easy to love with good rapport with the pastoral team. Another interesting aspect of his administration was his transparency. All of the ministry promotions were done consistent with the career path of the minister. What a marvelous experience to be supervised by a leader of the magnitude, skill, quality, and passion of the Reverend Antonio Collazo and to enjoy the company of the great Collazo-Lugo family!

The joy of friendship with Brother Collazo and his family was a wonderful blessing from God for our family. Praise God for the Collazo-Lugo family! Our love, gratitude, and respect to Sister Pérsida, Ligia, Totoño, Tita, Raquel, Tata and their extended families for sharing him with us. His work and achievements carry over into the present. Their results reach to eternity. We love and admire you all!

Epilogue

As God determines, following a life filled with ministerial and personal achievements in Puerto Rico as well as in the United States, on January 7, 1989, at age 78, Reverend Antonio Collazo ceased his earthly work and entered the eternal mansions that his Savior had prepared for him as he had preached about so many times. Interestingly, on the day of his death, he was enjoying a full life. He had just returned from the home of his daughter Ligia when the moment of his final appointment with the Lord of heaven and earth unexpectedly arrived. As he had often played on his saxophone and sung the words, when his name was called up yonder, he joyfully responded. Thus ended 68 years of a life dedicated to the Lord of life, and 51 years of fruitful ministry in His vineyard. The article[1] below, that reviewed his life and ministry, was published that year in the Church of God Spanish periodical, *El Evangelio*.

The Reverend Antonio Collazo was born in Orocovis, Puerto Rico on May 7, 1910 and left to live with the Lord on January 7, 1989 at age 78. His parents were Juan A. Collazo and Carmen Rodríguez. Brother Tony, as he was affectionately known, grew up in a Christian

---

[1] "El Rdo. Antonio Collazo Ha Vencido La Muerte." *El Evangelio*, Volume XLV Number 6, April, May, June, 1989.

home and dedicated his life to the study and practice of the Word of God from an early age.

In spite of his love for the land of his birth, because of the Great Depression at the start of the 1930's, he decided to pack his belongings and travel to the United States in search of better opportunities. What he did not realize at the time was that the one who was to become his faithful lifelong partner remained in Puerto Rico. After some time, the young Pérsida Lugo traveled to New York City where they met, fell in love, and, on November 27, 1936, decided to join their lives before God and man in that city of skyscrapers.

That marriage produced five children. Ligia Douglas, who works as a financial administrator at IBM; Juan A. Collazo, an officer at the New York State Prison; Pérsida Collazo, writer of children's literature at Editorial Evangélica in Cleveland, TN; Raquel Collazo, an administrative analyst at IBM; and Rebecca Ramos, exporting manager at Pronto Cargo Company in Miami, Florida. He is also survived by his mother-in-law Isabel Lugo, son-in-law Eugene Douglas, 8 grandchildren, and four sisters.

Brother Collazo returned to Puerto Rico in 1938 to serve as an instructor at the Mizpa Bible Institute. He was ordained to the ministry in 1940 by Reverend Manuel T. Sánchez and named President of the newly organized First Pentecostal Church. He served as pastor of the largest church in the organization in that period until 1945, when, along with another 6 congregations, affiliated with the Church of God with general offices in Cleveland, TN. He continued pastoring the church that

152

was now known as the Church of God *Mission Board.* He was ordained again with this denomination and also served as supervisor of the Church of God on this charming Island. Upon his departure from Puerto Rico the church had grown from 5 churches to 65 strong congregations. He also organized what is today known as the Pentecostal Bible College. At that time, it functioned as a Bible Institute with classrooms located upstairs in the church building at Parada 22 in Santurce, Puerto Rico. The Institute began with six students and today boasts a student body of approximately 500. It is accredited by the Association of Theological Schools to confer bachelor's Degrees and is an extension of the School of Theology of our denomination.

In 1958 Brother Collazo was transferred to New York City to serve as the first Hispanic overseer of the Church of God in the United States. He had oversight of the Eastern Spanish District that encompassed all of the territory east of the Mississippi River. He remained in this post until 1970 when he was reassigned to supervise the South Central Spanish District with offices in San Antonio, Texas. His ministry in the Eastern Spanish District was so fruitful that it became financially self-sufficient and no longer needed assistance from the General Offices. While doing the work of the Lord in the various states where he was assigned, he also served as a member of the Church of God World Missions Board, the first Hispanic to fill that position. Brother Collazo continued in this role until 1976 when he retired from full-time ministry, not because he was finished with ministry, which was his life. He never failed to provide a word of counsel or preach the Gospel

Epilogue

when asked by a pastor or overseer. An example of this was when, in 1983, Reverend Cecil Knight asked him to return to active ministry because there was a need for someone of his stature and experience to serve as Overseer of the North Central Spanish District in Lansing Michigan. Brother Collazo gladly accepted and served in this capacity for a year.

One of his greatest dreams was to obtain the Bachelor of Science degree. Taking advantage of the opportunity after retirement, he enrolled at the State University of New York in New Paltz and, in 1980 at age 70 he received his degree while graduating with honors. That same year the Hispanic Institute of Ministry in Houston, Texas conferred on him the honorary degree of Doctor of Divinity. The following year he was certified by the state of New York to teach in the school system.

Tony Collazo has overcome death! We say this because his legacy and work continue through all of those ministers, missionaries, educators, and lay leaders whose lives were touched and changed by the example and spiritual guidance of this man of God. His family, friends, and colleagues are witnesses of a triumphant life in Christ.

The physical loss of Brother Tony leaves us with broken hearts because we no longer have him here with us, but that wonderful day is coming when we will all be gathered with the saints worshipping our God for eternity. So, we know that his present loss for us is ultimately a gain for as the Apostle Paul reminded: "So now also Christ will be magnified in my body, whether by life or by death. For to me, to live *is* Christ, and to die *is* gain" (Philippians 1:20-21 NIV).

On the one hand, this beautiful eulogy by the editor of *El Evangelio* offered a final farewell to our beloved Brother Tony in April 1989. The article presents an extraordinary summary of the life of a giant of the faith. Today, on the other hand, with this biography 28 years later, I have sought to reconstruct with a few strokes of the brush a ministry model for those many that did not have the opportunity to know Brother Tony. In the same way, hopefully those who knew him and have read these words will derive joy at having identified with him in some of its pages.

I close this trip through the life and ministry of Reverend Antonio Collazo with a brief postscript and some final thoughts on the project. Many thanks for joining me on this interesting and revealing journey. Turn the page to enjoy a perfect ending!

Postscript

In recent months I have paused my work on the series *100 Años Después* to write a biography of this giant of the faith known as Antonio Collazo, "Brother Tony." The truth is that this has been a very enjoyable project. When I started, I knew it would be so but did not imagine the extent to which was. I reviewed historical documents and interviewed "living" documents. Carmen and I traveled to many places to interview many persons who had been close to Brother Tony. I sat with his widow, Sister Pérsida and her daughters Ligia, Pérsida (Tita), Raquel, and Rebecca (Tata) as well as her son Juan Antonio (Totoño). It has been an emotional journey to look beyond his exterior façade to the thoughts, feelings, and actions of this minister of God. Certainly, as is true of all humans, he was not perfect. If I were interviewing him at this moment, he would acknowledge that and likely point out he would have done differently if given the opportunity. However, without a doubt, he was a man of uncommon grace, who, within his human limitations, always strove to maintain integrity between his faith and conduct. His family, colleagues in ministry, those he supervised, and his friends all attest to that reality.

It is because of the statements outlined above that I have come to more closely know a man I admired from a distance. The first time I saw Brother Tony was at my church in the Chapero district of the Caimito neighborhood in Rio Piedras, Puerto Rico sometime around 1957. That evening my small church was holding a business meeting. I was barely 15 years old and yet participated in the service and business meeting that followed. Back then there was always a time of devotion before the business session. Brother Tony arrived early and sat where the musicians usually sat. I saw that he had a large black case with him. He took a saxophone out of the case and began to get it ready. That night he was the only musician in the church. He accompanied the all singing during the devotion period. Then we moved to the church business meeting. Our pastor at the time was Vicente Valcárcel who was elderly and ill. The church wanted a change in pastor and Brother Tony listened to everyone who had something to say. I do not remember his decision with regard to the pastor that day. I do remember that later on a new pastor, Alberto Camacho, arrived at the church. That was my first encounter with Brother Tony.

Later, in 1964 when I left to study at Lee Bible College, I stopped in New York first and had a brief visit with him at his office on the second floor of the church at Third Avenue and 116th Street. My next encounters with Brother Tony were during my studies in Cleveland, Tennessee in 1964-1966. Every time he visited Cleveland he made it a point to visit the Hispanic students who studied at Lee. Later on, I heard him preach on several occasions when he visited Puerto Rico or when serving as interpreter for Billy Graham and the Church of God leaders from the US. While he served as interim Overseer of the North Central Spanish region in 1983, I attended their convention and spent some time with him. I believe that was the last time I shared any close-up time with this renowned apostle to the Hispanic community in the United States and Latin America.

My most recent encounter with Brother Tony, by means of this project, has been refreshing. The experience of hearing the testimony of persons from different periods, with different backgrounds, and varying ages has projected a consistent image of this man of God and had been very thrilling and educational. The Bible says: "so that 'every matter may be established by the testimony of two or three witnesses'" (Matthew 18:16 NIV). That Biblical principle has proven true in the various accounts of the life of Brother Tony. The testimony of many confirms the impact of the life and ministry of Brother Tony on the lives of thousands of people who were reached by the ministry of this apostle to the Hispanic world.

It seems to me that the challenge we contemporary leaders of the church face is to emulate the faith of champions like Brother Tony. Fortunately, the Church of God has many champions whose faith is exemplary and worthy of imitating. For now, with much appreciation and pleasure, I have shared the story of the life and ministry of Reverend Antonio Collazo: A true Apostle! I hope that many will be enlightened and blessed with account of the life and ministry of a humble man filled with the grace of God!

Wilfredo Estrada Adorno

July 13, 2017

Flying at 33,00 feet from Miami to Charlotte

Bibliography

Betancourt, Esdras. *En el espíritu y poder de pentecostés: Historia de la iglesia de Dios hispana en Estados Unidos*. Cleveland, TN: CEL Publicaciones, 2016.

———. Interview by Wilfredo Estrada-Adorno, May 8, 2017.

Bonilla, Antonino. Interview by Wilfredo Estrada-Adorno, June 4, 2017.

Burgeño, Fidencio. Interview by Wilfredo Estrada-Adorno, June 4, 2017.

"C. E. and Helen French." *The Church of God Evangel*, October 12, 1946.

Collazo, Antonio. "Avanza Desde Aquí," n.d. Sermon notes of Antonio Collazo.

———. "Bendice Alma Mía a Jehová," enero 1968. Sermon notes of Antonio Collazo.

———. "Despierta El Don de Dios." *El Evangelio*, October 1976.

———. "El Nacimiento Virginal de Cristo." *El Evangelio*, 1982.

———. "El Velo Roto," n.d. Sermon notes of Antonio Collazo.

———. "Estadísticas de Junio, Iglesia de Dios Territorio Sur Central Hispano." *El Noticiero*, June 1976.

Bibliography

———. "Evangelismo En El Hogar." *El Evangelio*, November 1976.

———. "La Inspiración Verbal de La Biblia." *El Evangelio*, February 1982.

———. "La Sangre de Cristo Jesús," enero 1968. Sermon notes of Antonio Collazo.

———. "Pentecostés Con Propósito." *El Evangelio*, June 1976.

———. "Poder de Dios Y Con Los Hombres." *El Evangelio*, September 2011.

———. "Preparados Para Un Gran Encuentro," enero 1958. Sermon notes of Antonio Collazo.

———. "Regocijo Para El Atribulado," n.d. Sermon notes of Antonio Collazo.

Collazo Douglas, Ligia. Interview by Wilfredo Estrada-Adorno, agosto 2017.

Collazo Pagán, Persida. Interview by Wilfredo Estrada-Adorno, agosto 2017.

Collazo, Raquel. Interview by Wilfredo Estrada-Adorno, agosto 2017.

Collazo, Rebecca. Interview by Wilfredo Estrada-Adorno, agosto 2017.

"El Rdo. Antonio Collazo Ha Vencido La Muerte." *El Evangelio*, n.d.

"Eras de La Mies: La Iglesia de Dios Avanza Al Este Del Mississippi." *El Evangelio*, March 1965.

Estrada-Adorno, Wilfredo. *¡Oh poder pentecostal!: Adolescencia temprana madurez e impacto social del pentecostalismo puertorriqueño (1926-1966)*. Vol. 3. 100 años después. Trujillo Alto, PR: Ediciones Guardarraya, 2017.

León, Víctor De. *The Silent Pentecostals: A Biographical History of the Pentecostal Movement among the Hispanics in the Twentieth Century*. Taylor, SC: Faith Printing Company, 1979.

Lugo Collazo, Juan Antonio Collazo. Interview by Wilfredo Estrada-Adorno, agosto 2017.

Lugo Collazo, Pérsida. Interview by Wilfredo Estrada-Adorno, May 19, 2017.

Lugo, Juan L. *Pentecostés En Puerto Rico: La Vida de Un Misionero*. San Juan, PR: Puerto Rico Gospel Press, 1951.

Macías, Ignacio. Interview by Wilfredo Estrada-Adorno, June 5, 2017.

Montañez, Felipe. Interview by Wilfredo Estrada-Adorno, June 5, 2017.

Bibliography

Navas, Miguel. *Compendio de Minutas de La Iglesia de Dios "M. B." de Puerto Rico*. Saint Just, PR, 1969.

Osborn, T. L. *Personal Diary Notes: The Ponce, Puerto Rico Crusade and Its Significance*. Ladonna Osborn, 2007.

Pagán Lozada, Víctor M. Interview by Wilfredo Estrada-Adorno, agosto 2017.

Pérez, Manuel. Entrevista telefónica con el reverendo Manuel Pérez Sánchez el martes 9 de mayo de 2017. Interview by Wilfredo Estrada-Adorno, May 9, 2017.

Robles, Pascual, and Gladys Navas. Interview by Wilfredo Estrada-Adorno, June 5, 2017.

Santiago, Helen. *El pentecostalismo de Puerto Rico: Al compás de una fe autóctona (1916-1956)*. Trujillo Alto, PR: Helen Santiago, 2015.

Stoppe, Henry G. "A Short Biography of Brother Collazo: Missionary and Assistant Overseer of Puerto Rico." *The Lighted Pathway*, October 1945.

———. "A Short Biography of Brother Collazo: Missionary and Assistant Overseer of Puerto Rico." *The Lighted Pathway*, October 1945.

Attachments

APPEARS IN *WHO'S WHO*

WHO'S WHO IN RELIGION is a book that lists biographical sketches of individuals who have demonstrated excellence in the religious arena of their various creeds and religious denominations. According to the editors, the criteria for selection of those included is merit on the basis of their outstanding work in a particular area of service

Among those selected for the first edition of WHOS WHO was the Reverend Antonio Collazo (Pg. 117), Overseer of the Central Spanish District in the United States. The information published in the book was edited by Marquis Who's Who, Inc., with offices in Chicago, IL USA, and is included below.

Collazo, Antonio, minister. Born in Ponce, Puerto Rico on June 13, 1910. The son of Juan Antonio Collazo and Carmen Rodriguez. He studied at the Hispanic Bible Institute in California (1933-34). Married to Pérsida Lugo on November 17, 1936. Children: Ligia (wife of Luis Renta), Juan Antinio, Raquel (wife of F. Pacheco, Pérsida, and Rebecca (wife of Nicolás Ramos).

Ordained with the Church of God in 1940. Teacher at the Mizpa Bible Institute in Santurce, Puerto Rico (1938-1940). President of the First Pentecostal Church in Santurce, Puerto Rico (1940-1945). Pastor of the Church of God in Santurce (1944-1958). Overseer Eastern Spanish District in the United States (1970 -). Member of the World Missions Board of the Church of God

Bibliography

(1966-1974); of the Hispanic Institute of Ministry (1974 -).

He has been honored by the Church of God Eastern Spanish District (1962); Puerto Rico (1970). Member and co-founder of the Association of the Christian Child.

ADDITIONAL ATTACHMENTS ARE PHOTOCOPIES OF VARIOUS DOCUMENTS.

THE LAST ATTACHMENT INCLUDES THE FOLLOWING WORDS AS AN INTRODUCTION TO THE COPY.

Copy of the hymn *Mi Testimonio*, submitted by Sister Dora Hilda Colón, member of the Church of God *Mission Board* of Pugnado in Manatí.